Mollie's Legacy of Love

Edited by
Theresa Baldini, MM, and Madeline McHugh, MM
Maryknoll Contemplative Community

Mollie's Legacy of Love
is dedicated to the Teresians,
those heroic women who came to Maryknoll
between 1912 and 1920.

They came with open and generous hearts
to serve, as a community,
the needs of the newly-founded Maryknoll Society,
particularly the work on The Field Afar magazine,
believing that the path would lead them
to the deepest and truest of themselves ~
missioners in their own right!

May their lives and commitment
continue to inspire all
in the Maryknoll Family and beyond!

છ છ છ

January 6, 1912 to February 1, 1920
Sisters who entered before the Maryknoll Sisters were canonically recognized.
Adapted from Research prepared by Kathleen (Kathy) Magee, MM

NAME	ENTERED	PROFESSED	WITHDREW
1912			
1-Mary Xavier (Mary Louise) Wholean	1/6/1912	1917-Private Vows	
2-Mary Teresa (Sara Teresa) Sullivan	1/6/1912	2/15/1921*	
3-Mary Augustine (Mary) Dwyer	1/6/1912	-----	4/5/1916
4-Mary Theophane (Nora Frances) Shea	4/17/1912	2/15/1921*	
5-Mary Joseph (Mary Josephine) [Mollie] Rogers	9/9/1912	2/15/1921*	
6-Mary Gemma (Margaret Anne) Shea	9/9/1912	4/13/1921*	
7-Anna Maria (Anne Agnes) Towle	10/6/1912	2/15/1921*	
1913			
8-Josephine Mathias	2/19/1913	-----	3/3/1913
9-Mary Dominic (Mary Virginia) Foylan	2/27/1913	-----	12/16/1918
10-Mary Bernadette (Maria Francina) Hoar	7/6/1913	-----*	8/8/1921
1914			
11-Mary Catherine (Katherine Gertrude) Fallon	5/14/1914	2/15/1921*	
12-Mary Ambrose (Mary Laetitia) Crawford	9/15/1914	2/15/1921*	
13-Carmellia Elder	11/2/1914	-----	4/3/1915
14-Mary Francis (Elsie Frances St. Claire) Davis	12/28/1914	2/15/1921*	
1915			
15-Julia Trabucco	5/15/1915	-----	6/30/1915
16-Margaret Mary Kelleher	6/19/1915	-----	9/6/1915
17-Mary Elizabeth Regan	8/28/1915	-----	11/3/1915
18-Mary Agatha (Ellen Frances) Davin	10/15/1915	2/15/1921*	
1916			
19-Mary Anthony (Nora) Conway	1/22/1916	2/15/1921*	
20-Mary Dolores (Mary Ann) Cruise	1/31/1916	2/15/1921*	
21-Marie Magdalen (Mary Magdalen) Doelger	5/24/1916	3/19/1921*	
22-Mary Rose (Anna Rose) Leifels	9/19/1916	2/15/1921	
23-Mary Aloysius (Alice Marie) McDonald	10/25/1916	3/19/1921	
24-Mary Patrick (Elinor) Maher	11/1/1916	2/15/1921	
25-Mary Elizabeth (Anna Mary Regina) Thompson	11/5/1916	2/15/1921	

> * On July 16, 1918, the thirteen Teresians, who had been there the longest,
> made private vows to Father Charles J. Callan, OP,
> a scripture scholar at the Seminary.

NAME	ENTERED	PROFESSED	WITHDREW
1917			
26-Margaret Mary (Katherine A.) Slattery	2/2/1917	2/15/1921	
27-Mary Paul (Grace Anselma) McKenna	7/10/1917	2/15/1921	
28-Ruth Conover	7/18/1917	-----	8/20/1917
29-Stella Rahl	7/24/1917	-----	8/27/1917
30-Mary Michael (Mary Ann) Conlin	8/27/1917	2/15/1921	
31-Mary Thomas (Bridgid Mary) Bresnahan	8/31/1917	2/15/1921	
32-Olga Nicolajevona Bjerring	11/3/1917	-----	12/31/1917
1918			
33-Mary John (Mary Ellen) [Troy] Cahill	2/12/1918	2/15/1921	
34-Mary Agnes (Anna Louise Colette) McCabe	2/23/1918	-----	11/27/1918
35-Mary Rita (Elizabeth) Bodkin	6/7/1918	2/15/1921	
36-Mary Immaculata (Irene Cecilia) Carlin	6/1918	-----	4/7/1919
37-Mary James (Louise Regis) Rogers	7/6/1918	2/15/1921	
38-Mary Philomena (Catherine) [Kate] Flanagan	8/14/1918	2/15/1921	
39-Mary Gerard (Anna Catherine) Gallagher	9/17/1918	4/13/1921	
1919			
40-Mary Lawrence (Bridget Teresa) Foley	3/24/1919	8/4/1921	
41-Marie de Lourdes (Anna Mary) Bourguignon	5/18/1919	8/4/1921	
42-Mary Stephen (Julia) O'Donnell	10/4/1919	8/4/1921	
43-Mary Mercedes (Mary Veronica) Cusak	9/11/1919	8/4/1921	
44-Mary Peter (Beatrice Mary) Duggan	10/7/1919	8/4/1921	
45-Mary Barbara (Clara Barbara) Froehlich	10/14/1919	8/4/1921	
46-Mary Teresita (Jane) O'Donnell	10/14/1919	8/4/1921	
47-Mary Imelda (Mary Crescentia) [Savage] Sheridan	10/14/1919	8/4/1921	
48-Mary Ursula (Gertrude) Kenkel	11/15/1919	8/4/1921	
49-Mary Carmel (Mary Catherine) Murphy	11/17/1919	8/4/1921	
50-Mary Veronica (Rose Apollonia) Hartman	12/7/1919	8/4/1921	
51-Mary Columba (Elizabeth Helena) Tarpey	12/7/1919	8/4/1921	
1920			
52-Mary Clare (Gertrude Virginia) Miltenberger	2/1/1920	8/4/1921	
53-Mary Monica (Alice Agnes) Moffatt	2/1/1920	8/4/1921	

40 sisters remained and
13 women were called to another way of life.

೮೧ ೮೧ ೮೧

Contents

෨ ෨ ෨

Introduction

*For our Introduction,
we share the reflections
Sister Janice McLaughlin, MM,
President of the Maryknoll
Sisters, gave when
Mother Mary Joseph was
inducted into the National
Women's Hall of Fame in Seneca
Falls, NY, on October 12, 2013.*

If Mother Mary Joseph Rogers were standing here today, I believe she would say that we celebrate not only an individual, or the community that she founded, but that we honor women everywhere who strive to make the world a better place for all. Such was her inclusive, worldwide vision. I rejoice that many members of the Rogers' family are with us today as well as members of the extended Maryknoll family.

Last year Maryknoll Sisters celebrated our 100th anniversary – 100 years of living out Mother Mary Joseph's vision of compassionate service throughout the world. Beginning our second century of mission, we continue to reach out to those in need with her unprejudiced, worldwide heart.

Mary Josephine Rogers, known affectionately as Mollie, came from a large and loving Irish Catholic family in Boston. The Rogers' home was a gathering place for classmates and friends who came to sing around the piano, dance, play games and enjoy good food and good stories around the table. Mollie brought this family spirit of sharing, fun and laughter to Maryknoll.

She developed an international outlook early in her life and an appreciation of diversity. Her collection of books and dolls from around the world exposed her to a reality far removed from Boston. Looking back on her life, she said: *"....from an early age I was keenly alive to the existence of little sisters and brothers in far off lands quite different from myself in race, color and creed."*[1]

This open and worldwide heart was visible in her valedictory address at her graduation from West Roxbury High School in 1900. She began her speech on the subject of *"Toleration"* by quoting St. Augustine:

> *In what is essential, unity; in what is indifferent, liberty;*
> *and in all things, charity.*[2]

Unity, liberty, charity ~ these would be among the guiding principles of the missionary congregation that she founded in 1912.

She was only 29 years of age when she took this major step. Nine years later she sent the first six Maryknoll Sisters to China. They pioneered a new approach to mission, going out two by two to live in the homes of poor villagers for weeks at a time, sharing their way of life with all its hardships. Referring to this experiment and other innovative mission practices in Latin America and Africa, author Penny Lernoux stated: *"Long before the 1960's when religious orders made a 'preferential option for the poor,' the Maryknoll Sisters were living it."*[3]

Mother Mary Joseph firmly believed that women could do much of the same work as priests and that American women had the stamina and determination to go anywhere in the world where they were needed. She imprinted her unique spirit on the community she founded. This spirit encompassed retaining one's individuality, something that was rare at a time of uniformity in religious life.

---

1 Mother Mary Joseph, "Mission Interest," 1941, MMA, (Box 1, Folder 6), quoted in Carr, Elizabeth, <u>The Spirituality of Mollie Rogers, Founder of the Maryknoll Sisters Congregation</u>, Maryknoll, 2012, p. 4.

2 Hendricks, Barbara, <u>As One Lamp Lights Another, The Life and Story of Mother Mary Joseph</u>, Maryknoll Sisters, 2013, p. 14. *(Further research has indicated that this quote is from St. Austin, not St. Augustine.)*

3 Lernoux, Penny, <u>Hearts on Fire</u>, Orbis Books, 2011 (centennial edition), p. 59.

She had a gift for explaining our vocation in clear, down-to-earth terms. Very simply she spoke of the Maryknoll spirit *"as being a reflection of the love of God – nothing more nor less than that – a reflection of the love of God."*[4] Ahead of her time, even in her approach to prayer, she turned to the women mystics for inspiration. Teresa of Avila, famous mystic and doctor of the church, became our patron.

Mother Mary Joseph urged us to be contemplatives in action and learn to live in the Presence of God. With an awareness of the demands our vocation would entail, she counseled us: *"If you have not cultivated the habit of speaking with God, you will find yourselves frightened and alone in a great desert. So learn to listen to God."*[5]

She had a grasp of world affairs and was open to taking risks when the need for our service was great. She, therefore, did not hesitate to send her sisters into dangerous situations where they might face imprisonment, deportation and even death. This was indeed the case in China, North Korea, Japan and the Philippines. In recent years, two of our sisters were murdered in El Salvador with two other church women.

Mother Mary Joseph taught us to respect other cultures and to be open to dialog with people of diverse beliefs. Educating our new members, she told them: *"Maryknoll does not go to turn Asiatics or Africans into Americans or Westerners....as far as customs go, we are the ones who do the changing over."*[6]

A zoologist by training, I believe that she would feel at home with the environmental movement and with efforts to promote sustainable development. Her interest in the arts led her to encourage members to develop their artistic, musical and dramatic talents where they would lend creativity to their endeavors.

She listed *"the saving grace of a sense of humor"*[7] among the qualities that should distinguish a Maryknoll Sister. Her own humor and sense of fun were contagious. She entertained new members with parties, games, outings and amusing stories of the early days and could laugh at herself.

---

4   Ibid, p. 3, # 7, 1932.

5   Ibid, 1930.

6   Mother Mary Joseph, Maryknoll History, January 29, 1948, p. 1456.

7   Constitutions, MMJ, 1935.

Looking back on her life she said: *"When I was a little girl, I used to dream of the time I would be rich enough to have a soda fountain in my own house."*[8] Instead, she introduced the custom of having ice cream sodas on October 15th, the feast of our patron, Teresa of Avila. I invite you to enjoy an ice cream soda in her honor this coming week – October 15th.

Though the world has changed drastically in the past century, Mother Mary Joseph's example continues to inspire us as we translate her words and deeds into contemporary action.

Today we serve in two dozen countries caring for orphans who have lost their parents to AIDS, engaging in inter-religious dialog, reaching out to victims of trafficking, accompanying migrants, advocating for the protection of the environment and offering peace education and trauma healing to victims of violence.[9]

We believe that Mother Mary Joseph's legacy lives on not only in the women who joined Maryknoll but in the thousands of people our lives have touched over the years. A graduate from one of our schools in the Philippines summed it up recently when she wrote:

> *They (Maryknoll Sisters) live on,*
> *if not in a national hall of fame like their founder,*
> *then in the hearts, minds and lives*
> *of those they taught and loved.*[10]

We give thanks for that legacy and for the honor of having Mother Mary Joseph Rogers join other prominent women leaders in this National Hall of Fame.

ഇ   ഇ   ഇ

---

8   Carr, Elizabeth, op cit, Mother Mary Joseph, Letter (to "My Dearest Sisters"), 17 July 1947, p. 5.

9   Woo, Carolyn, CNS September 2013, "From Just One Woman...of Faith".

10   Jimenez-David, Rina, "A Different Sort of Missionary," Philippine Daily Inquirer, August 12, 2013.

#1 ~ Mollie's Early Years

Mollie at four years of age.

Mollie Rogers was a woman who knew the daily functioning of a large family. The fourth of eight children born to Mary Josephine Plummer and Abraham Theobald Rogers on October 27, 1882, in Roxbury, Massachusetts, she was christened Mary Josephine Rogers on November 13, 1982, at St. Francis de Sales Church in Roxbury.

"When I was born," Mollie wrote, *"I was the first girl after three boys. My father, who worked in real estate, was so delighted he ran around from house to house in the neighborhood announcing the news. He was always inordinately proud of me. He used to sit on our front porch waving my report card in his hand. Then he would call out to the neighbors as they passed, 'Do you want to see Mollie's report card?' I used to feel like 6 cents."*

Mollie's Paternal Grandparents

Grandfather Patrick Rogers and Mary Dunn, both immigrants from Ireland to Canada, fell in love. When Patrick asked Mary if she would marry him, she answered, *"I will, when you take me and my sisters to Boston."* Her mother had died, leaving three younger sisters in her care. Grandfather Rogers was on his quiet way upward economically and politically, early to become a builder and a member of the Common Council, an investor in real estate and an outstanding taxpayer.

The sons of Patrick and Mary Dunn Rogers were Joseph, Francis and Mollie's father, Abraham. They walked in their father's shadow, protected by his stature from the cold winds that he had to face of anti-Catholic and anti-Irish sentiment. The brothers bonded together, never losing their sense of partnership.

Mollie's Maternal Grandparents

Grandmother Plummer had been Bridget Josephine Kennedy, a lovely young woman who had charmed William Gardner Plummer, who was a Calvinist. He not only married her, but did so in a Catholic ceremony. He loved his wife and as he grew older, his natural goodness overcame much of his earlier prejudice. However, when his own children were growing up, he gave in only reluctantly to his wife's gentle but unrelenting insistence that their children be allowed to practice their Catholic faith. Mollie's mother never forgot how it felt to be obliged to go to a neighbor's house to get dressed in the white dress and veil that she would wear to her First Communion.

Mollie's Younger Years

As a little girl Mollie had dreamed of being a missionary. She was moved by many influences ~ from her doll collection of different nations to the stories read to her by her father about neglected children, like Oliver Twist, and accounts later spelled out in the *Annals of the Holy Childhood* and the Propagation of the Faith.

"I was fortunate as a child," Mollie wrote, *"that from an early age I was keenly alive to the existence of little sisters and brothers in far off lands quite different from myself in race, color and creed."* She saw the world at a very early age as one family. Mollie had dreams, also, of growing up and owning a soda fountain to which she and all her friends could resort at will and without cost! A lively spirit pervaded Mollie's home. *"The kitchen in the old home was a large one,"* Mollie's cousin Francis Rogers reminisced, *"and was a great gathering place for all the young folks in the neighborhood, especially on a winter evening. I can see it now ~ filled with youngsters, doing a Virginia Reel or playing Blind Man's Bluff and Mollie at the stove getting molasses candy ready to pull or making a cake."*

Relatives in Politics

Mollie's childhood, with all its fascinations, was the breeding ground of a broad vision, embodied and articulated from her early school days. She was a schoolgirl in the 1880's when being Irish and Catholic could well cast one outside of Boston's social strata. Despite their immigrant status, the Rogers Family took its place in Boston's politics and education. Mollie's grandfather, Patrick Rogers, was the first Catholic in Boston elected to public office and Mollie followed in his footsteps in terms of leadership. She was a leader, even at home.

Her mother had frail health and, according to Francis Rogers, *"Mollie at an early age took over the management of the home and I can assure you that no one questioned her authority."*

Mollie's Family Life

Abraham, Mollie's father and the youngest of the three boys, had the largest family. He was completely devoted to his wife and immensely pleased with his eight children: William, Leo, Ned, Mollie, Elizabeth, Louise, John and Abe. After the death of his father Patrick in 1890, Abraham's mother divided her husband's legacy among her children and went to stay with each family. She spent a good bit of time with Abraham's family, as he had the most forbearing wife. Grandma had Mollie parade back and forth in front of her with a book on her head to improve her posture, as well as stopping by Mollie's room after she was in bed and putting a clothespin on Mollie's nose to make it more patrician. How long the clothespin stayed on after Grandma left the room was Mollie's secret! When Mollie was going on a date, Grandma said: *"Mollie, that boy you are going out with, what does his father do?"* Mollie responded, *"He is an iceman, Grandma."* Not hearing too well, Grandma said, *"Of course, I know he is a nice man, but what does he DO?"*

Mollie had already made a good escape with the son of a nice man! Often the dinner table at the Rogers' home in Jamaica Plain was set for twenty ~ the children all being welcome to invite friends home for supper. This family spirit Mollie would bring with her to Maryknoll.

There were undoubtedly good stories told around the Rogers' dining table, especially when Mollie's maternal uncle, George Plummer from Charlestown and a Salem sea captain, would come for dinner. In addition to stories and visions of great deeds and faraway places, Mollie's childhood was filled with the wonders of the country and of the earth beneath her feet.

Grammar and High School

In stair-step formation, the Rogers children moved through the local public schools. They were educated in a way that afforded them every possible opportunity to thrive at a time when Catholics in Boston were regarded, at best, as second-class citizens. At the grade school level, the boys attended Agasy; the girls, Bowditch. Mollie was confirmed by Archbishop John J. Williams of Boston on October 7, 1894, choosing the name *Frances,* at the Church of St Thomas, Jamaica Plain, MA.

When the children graduated from the ninth grade, boys and girls were reunited at West Roxbury High School. The high school offered a three-year course leading to a diploma, and for those interested and able, a fourth year of college preparation. All of the Rogers' children took this option. The program of studies was ambitious and the teachers were dedicated and demanding. The students were administered strong doses of history, English language, literature, mathematics and science, as well as, Latin, Greek and a modern language. Mollie learned French.

When the young Rogers gathered around the big table in the upper hall to settle down to their homework, Mollie always had time to help anyone wrestling with a difficulty, whether it was an arithmetic problem or a tough passage of French. Mollie always seemed to have time for other things besides studying, but she certainly did well at school. Her brother, Ned, was one of the business officers on the monthly *Clarion,* and Mollie was one of the editors. She also held class offices, was chosen for the debating team and the committee on dramatics, as well as becoming vice-president of the athletic association.

After her third year, Mollie was named valedictorian of her high school graduating class in June 1900. The subject of her speech was *Toleration,* and she began with the words: *"In what is essential, Unity; in what is indifferent, Liberty; in all things, Charity."* Mollie then took the optional fourth year for college preparation, receiving her diploma on June 25, 1901. Mollie's five brothers went to Harvard University, and Mollie followed her cousin, Anna Frances Rogers, to Smith College.

A Reflective Moment
1 - What qualities in Mollie ground us in
our Maryknoll Community spirit?
2 - How did I first experience my call to mission?

Resources
The above Reflections were adapted from:
Maryknoll's First Lady
by Jeanne Marie Lyons, MM,
and *The Spirituality of Mollie Rogers*
by Elizabeth Carr, Ph.D.

ॐ   ॐ   ॐ

Mollie at 29 years of age.

#2 ~ First Contact with Father James Anthony Walsh

A Mission Seed Planted

In the late nineteenth century, when Catholics in the United States had little awareness of world mission, Mollie's parents ensured through Sunday school that their children would grow up with some familiarity of the church's foreign mission activity. In the early 1940's Mollie, now Mother Mary Joseph, made notes of her recollections:

> *As a Catholic child, I was taught to pray for missioners and the children they were trying to teach about God, and to share with them the little store of money that was mine to spend as I liked. Being highly imaginative, I even visualized myself as a missionary going about doing good and converting whole cities. As I grew older, the day dreams faded, and beyond prayers and small contributions, I paid little heed to the souls for whom our Divine Savior thirsted.*

Smith College

With this kind of background Mollie began college studies at Smith College in Northampton, Massachusetts, in the fall of 1901. Although she had wanted to be a nurse, her father insisted she go to college. Almost from her first day at Smith, Mollie's early openness to the world and the peoples of the world was rekindled. The faith her parents had nurtured in her as a child blossomed in the encounters she had with other students. One of them questioned her one day about where she went in the mornings. *"To Mass,"* she replied, *"and yes, she really believed God came to her every morning in Holy Communion."* The student responded with a sudden rush of tears ~ if only she could believe that!

As a zoology student, Mollie earned the respect of Professor Harris Hawthorne Wilder, who would recommend her for graduate teaching and further study in the field. As an undergraduate, she participated in college activities, including the Chapel Choir, the Ancient Order of Hibernia (being called "Boodge O'Rogers" in the yearbook), the Biological Society and the College Mission Club.

The Student Volunteer Movement

Mollie came into close contact with the Protestant mission activities while at Smith. It is a well known fact that the mission activities of Protestants excelled throughout the entire 19th century. In 1904, as a Junior, Mollie dreamed about the future and what her part was to be in the betterment of the world. She would soon be a senior and a definite decision must be made. The pondering of these thoughts in her heart was broken by a crowd of excited girls who had just signed the Student Volunteer Pledge. Mollie was moved profoundly. It was a religious experience that she said she "*did not know how to describe,*" but that she would put it this way:

> *It was a June evening, still, warm, and sweet with the fragrance of the flowering campus. I was a junior in one of the largest non-sectarian colleges in the country, and as I walked slowly towards the Students' Building, I dreamed in the manner of every girl of that age about the future. These wholesome reveries were suddenly broken by shouts of joy as the great doors of the Students' Building were flung open and floods of light poured out upon the paths. A crowd of girls rushed out and, before I realized what was happening, a circle had been formed about five or six of them, and the stirring strains of 'Onward, Christian Soldiers' were winging themselves over the campus.*

> *I soon learned that these girls had just signed the Student Volunteer Pledge and that the following September would see them all on the way to China as foreign missionaries to teach in the mission schools or work in the hospitals. Everybody in the college knew what the Student Volunteer Pledge meant, but this was our first experience in the actual offering of the girls, and they were the college's best. All were jubilant about it.*

> *Something, I do not know how to describe it, happened within me. I forgot my errand; I was no longer mindful of the beauty and joy about me. I passed quickly through the campus, out of the campus grounds, and across the street to the Church where, before Jesus in the tabernacle, I measured my faith and the expression of it by the sight I had just witnessed.*

I was Catholic and I had known from childhood that there were foreign mission societies that needed help; I had even had idle visions of working for the salvation of souls. The fact was that I had done nothing....From that moment I had work to do, little or great, God alone knew.

Newman Club at Smith

Mollie's imaginative childhood dreams of *"being a missionary and going about doing good"* were beginning to take shape as the work she knew she had to do. That very year she would actually begin that work, when in her junior year at Smith she led an extracurricular study class on Catholic missions. Then in her senior year in 1904, Mollie was the leader and sustaining spirit of an organization of Catholic students, which promoted frequent reception of the sacraments, generosity to Catholic missions, a fine upholding of the Catholic reputation in the classroom, social circles, and local welfare work of Smith College. She inspired others with a lifelong zeal for God's service. This group of Catholic students who met on Friday evenings would become the Newman Club at Smith, with Mollie its first president.

Boston Normal School

Mollie completed her college studies at Smith and received her Bachelor of Arts Degree in Zoology on June 18, 1905. In the fall, she enrolled at Boston Normal School in a special section for college graduates and at the end of the year received her teaching certificate.

The Development of a Catholic Mission Group

After her graduation from Boston Normal School, upon the recommendation of Professor Wilder, Mollie accepted in the fall of 1906 an invitation by Smith College to return on a fellowship as a Laboratory Demonstrator in the Zoology Department. At the same time, she was chosen to be a 'house mother' at White Lodge, a recognized position at one of the select off-campus residences for senior students.

Mollie was hardly settled back before she was challenged by Miss Elizabeth Deering Hanscom, a professor of English and the faculty advisor of *The Smith College Association for Christian Work,* to organize some kind of religious activity for the Catholic students. Feeling incompetent and unprepared for a Bible study group, Mollie suggested a Mission Study Club. With Miss Hanscom's encouragement, Mollie decided to follow the foreign mission interest which was assuming a greater hold in her spirit, heart and mind. Forty-eight young women signed up to be part of the Mission Study Club.

On the way back to her residence hall, Mollie, not altogether sure of herself, was so unnerved by this commitment that she nearly changed her mind. She knew there were few resources available, and she would need a lot of material, if indeed, she would be able to gather a group of Catholic girls in a mission study club at all! In this frame of mind, she consulted Father Michael Welch, her confessor and curate at St. Mary's Church, probably half-hoping he would dissuade her. Instead, he encouraged her to contact Father James Anthony Walsh, director of the Society for the Propagation of the Faith in Boston since 1903.

Mollie's Letter to Father Walsh

Mollie wrote to Father James A. Walsh in October 1906, outlining the content of her weekly discussion sessions at Smith and asking him for information on the following:

1) The preparation of priests and nuns for mission work,
2) Mission Orders,
3) The nature of the work, and
4) The collection and distribution of funds.

The letter which Mollie wrote to Father Walsh
revealed clearly her own deep intent.

The particular motive of these classes is to inspire girls to do actual mission work when they leave college. She concluded ....*Will you kindly tell me where I can get any information (in English, French or Latin) bearing on these lines of thought? And will you kindly send me some pamphlets concerning the Propagation of the Faith? Who knows but that the little work we do here may be the beginning of greater efforts in later life.*

Father Walsh's Response

A prompt answer came from Father Walsh, dated October 20, 1906:

"Far from bothering me, your appeal gives me great pleasure in the thought that you will interest the Catholic girls of Smith College in the great work of Catholic Foreign Missions." He commended the points for discussion which she had proposed and added another of his own: *"The martyr spirit of our age."* He sent her a supply of materials which he thought should be of help for the group; and, for herself, a copy of the *Life of Theophane Venard* as a gift. He closed his letter saying: *"I shall look upon it as a privilege and a pleasure to assist you in the effort which you are making and for which Almighty God will give you some reward through the prayers and sacrifices of those whom you are thereby helping."*

Carefully listing the materials which he was sending her, he moved on to the difficulty he experienced in writing on the subject on which his mind and heart were so full. He invited her to visit him so that he might instruct her personally. In the meantime with the passage of each week, he would send both materials and pictures to her. Mollie no longer had any fears for her class as she longed for the day to meet him in person.

Encounter with Father Walsh

Mollie Rogers made her first visit to see Father Walsh in person during the Christmas holidays in 1906. The impression of that meeting remained vivid all her life. She never ceased to recall it. It marked the beginning of her lifetime cooperation and friendship with Father, the one whom God chose with a gentle breath to fan into a living flame in her soul *"the already lighted spark of apostolic fire."*

> *I found him,* Mother Mary Joseph wrote many years later, *at his headquarters on Union Park Street, opposite the Cathedral. Such a surprising ready-to tumble-down place it was! Narrow, rickety stairs and a dark hall led to the 'rookery,' as he called his office, and it was with a sense of relief that I saw in the sun's revealing light a room lined with books, here and there on the wall bright splotches of color, a large desk, on the table beside it, a globe, and at the desk, smiling a welcome, the Director himself.*

The encounter of these two persons constituted a then unknown point of an inherent future, Maryknoll. Each detail of this first meeting was important to Mollie, his office, his surroundings, his accumulation of mission materials. Of significant importance on the day of that famous visit to him was the fact that Mollie saw the galley sheets of the first copy of *The Field Afar,* his new Catholic mission magazine, to be published January, 1907.

Mollie recorded this peak moment
of the experience of her visit:

> *I realized, of course, that Father was very busy and I said to him, "Well I must be going now." "Oh, no," he said, "you sit down, I am trying to form an opinion of you!" He always said afterward that he really never could have said anything so rude. "Well," I said, "you did, and I was very uncomfortable." But anyway I stayed and as I was leaving he said, "I think you and I are going to be very good friends."*

When Mollie left Father Walsh's office, she took along letters and articles to translate from French into English for future use in *The Field Afar*. For the following years, she became the nameless translator for *The Field Afar* behind many contributions by French missioners.

Mission Apostolate of The Field Afar

From 1907 until 1911, Mollie gave all her spare time to work with Father Walsh at the Society for the Propagation of the Faith Office (SPF) in Boston. Upon completing her second year as a Laboratory Demonstrator at Smith in 1908, she transferred to a Boston city school, primarily to collaborate with Father Walsh on a daily basis. The Boston location brought her closer to the mission work which now held first place in her life. Mollie's work was extensive with the translations to be made, editing to be done, topics to be developed into articles, any activity connected with the publication of *The Field Afar*. Mollie's life became absorbed in the mission apostolate of *The Field Afar*.

Nora Shea who became Sister M. Theophane

Father Walsh's secretary, Miss Donovan, wanted to be a Missionary Sister, and was entering a new missionary community near French Quebec. On the third Tuesday of the month, Father Walsh used to attend a promoters' meeting of the Society for the Propagation of the Faith made up of dedicated lay people. Through a faithful lay woman promoter whose accounts were beautifully done, he learned that a young woman named Nora Shea did the accounts for her and Nora was out of work. The promoter asked if Father could do anything for her and he responded that she come to see him.

Nora (Honora Frances), who was born on March 2, 1880, was the fifth child in a family of eight children. Her widowed mother had to work from dawn to dusk in one of the Massachusetts mills. Nora carried many responsibilities at home and always had a happy disposition.

By the first week of February 1909, Nora was working for Father Walsh. Two days after, when it came time for Miss Donovan to leave, she gave last minute instructions to Nora. Running down the steps, she paused and called back to Nora, "*Oh, you will be all right. Just pray to St. Jude. He is hanging on the wall there. He will do everything for you!*"

Mollie and Nora

A brighter day dawned for Nora when Mollie came to the office to help out. She knew where everything was and how everything was done. Nora's heart was Mollie's from that time on! Nora felt that altogether Mollie was a rather more empowering co-worker than St. Jude, with all due respect to him! By the spring of 1911, Mollie along with Nora Shea were following closely and facilitating the efforts of Fathers Walsh and Price to establish a foreign mission seminary in America.

Together these two women assumed more and more responsibility for the publication work connected with *The Field Afar*. At the same time, Fathers Walsh and Price moved a proposal for a foreign mission seminary to the agenda of the Archbishops' Meeting held on April 23, 1911, at the Catholic University in Washington, D.C. While Father Price paced the hall outside the meeting room of the archbishops in Washington, Father Walsh worked in his Boston office. When word came from Father Price that the proposal was *unanimously approved*, Father Walsh, Mollie and Nora, were the first to know!

Papal Approval

On May 31, 1911, Mollie and Nora took complete responsibility for the publication of *The Field Afar* as Fathers Walsh and Price sailed for Rome. Mollie, upon whom Father Walsh had come to rely heavily, applied her skills to oversee all the editorial work. Nora took care of the business end. Together, they heard that on June 29, the Feast of Sts. Peter and Paul, Cardinal Gotti had told Fathers Walsh and Price that the foreign mission society had papal approval.

Mollie and Nora were responsible for meeting the printer's deadlines for the publication of *The Field Afar* during those summer months until Fathers Walsh and Price returned in September. It was their privilege to put out the first two issues announcing the creation of the Catholic Foreign Mission Society of America and a Foreign Mission Seminary.

First Significant Event of Mollie's Life

Years later Mollie recorded outstanding events of her life regarding her mission vocation. She reflected on the first significant one as:

> *Going to Smith College where I saw the active work of Protestants for the missions. This led to my forming a mission study class at college; this was the immediate avenue to Father Walsh to whom I wrote in October of 1906, an event that marked the beginning of our friendship and cooperation.*

This was, in fact, what constituted
her first decisive step
toward the founding of the Maryknoll Sisters.

Just a Postscript
Sister M. Theophane (Nora Shea)

Since Mollie and Nora were close friends from the beginning, we share this meaningful excerpt from Mother Mary Joseph's Eulogy on Sister M. Theophane, who died from cancer on April 22, 1940:

> *There are flowers that show forth their beauty during the day and, as shadows lengthen, fold their petals in sleep to open them again only with the rising of the sun. Kindred to that loveliness was the soul of our dear Sister M. Theophane....She was quietly active, genuinely humble, gently firm, endowed with rare and sparkling humor....*

> *Her natural gifts seemed to irradiate her wasting form and to draw us to her as if in hope of absorbing something of her exquisite nobility of soul....her spirit still broods over us in loving, prayerful watchfulness.*

A Reflective Moment
1 - How does Mollie's journey evoke faith,
challenge and creativity in us?
2 - As Mollie empowered Nora Shea and so many others,
how do we empower others?

Resources
The above Reflections were adapted from:
To the Uttermost Parts of the Earth
by Camilla Kennedy, MM,
Maryknoll's First Lady by Jeanne Marie Lyons, MM,
Maryknoll in China by Jean-Paul Wiest,
On the Threshold of the Future
by Claudette LaVerdiere, MM,
The Spirituality of Mollie Rogers
by Elizabeth E. Carr, Ph.D., and
A Pictorial History by Sister Mary Francis Louise, MM.

ಬಲ   ಬಲ   ಬಲ

January 6, 1912
Left to Right: Mary Augustine Dwyer,
Sara Teresa Sullivan and Mary Louise Wholean.

Mary Louise Wholean
(Sister M. Xavier)

In 1904, when Mary Louise was a student at Wellesley College, she heard Father Walsh speak about foreign missions in a nearby parish church at Natick, MA, and she spoke with him afterwards. There was no other communication till September 1911, when Father Walsh found two letters from Mary Louise after he returned from Rome with the permission to start the Catholic Foreign Mission Seminary with Father Price. Mary Louise asked in her letters if there were any way in which she could serve the cause of mission. Father Walsh wrote to her that day in the Pennsylvania town where she was teaching, inviting her to come to see him.

She made a quick trip to Boston. Her first words were: *"I do not know why I have come, or what I can do, but something has been urging me for several years to give my life-work to the interests of the foreign missions."* Father Walsh learned to his surprise that Mary Louise had not heard of the existence of *The Field Afar* and knew nothing about the newly projected Society. The Holy Spirit had inspired her! Father made it clear that he could offer her only the opportunity to serve with no assurance that she would ever be a sister. Mary Louise was satisfied under any conditions. She had a good grasp of languages: French, Italian and German, which were especially helpful in translating missioners' letters for articles in *The Field Afar*.

As early as March 19, 1912, Mary Louise felt a peculiar pain in her side. Surgery on April first confirmed that she had cancer and that she might have only six or seven years to live. Although offered the option to return home, she chose to stay with the group and to contribute her services for as long as she could.

Succeeding surgeries and treatments enabled her to participate actively in the life and work of Maryknoll up to within two months of her death. She came to accept pain as a normal companion. Mary Louise wrote the Teresian Diary from 1912-1916, giving us a wonderful glimpse into those precious early days. Among Mollie's duties was being the infirmarian and she lovingly cared for Mary Louise throughout her illness.

In early February 1917, Mary Louise's mother sat at her bedside reading the February *Field Afar*. Mary Louise's eyes turned toward the paper and asked if it could be read to her. Her mother said she was looking for something interesting to read, and Mary Louise whose death was imminent, said, *"Why, it is all interesting!"* On February 19, 1917, Mary Louise, who chose the name, Sister M. Xavier, died peacefully at St. Teresa's Lodge, the first Maryknoller to die.

Sara Teresa Sullivan
(Sister M. Teresa)

Sara Teresa was born in County Kerry, Ireland, in 1874, and came to the States in 1879. She attended schools in Nashua, NH, and a business school in Boston, MA. For twelve years she was secretary to the Dean of the Medical College at Harvard University. Hearing a sermon by Father Thomas F. Price, her mission interest was kindled. In September 1911, she agreed to do typing for Father James A. Walsh, and in October she left the Dean's office at Harvard Medical School. Sara came to 242 Dover Street in Jamaica Plain several times a week to help Nora Shea, Father Walsh's secretary, who later became Sister M. Theophane. This was a room rented in the same place where the Washington Press printed *The Field Afar*. Sara was appalled at the dingy, noisy storeroom which Nora insisted upon calling an office. She found typing 8,000 names for the next issue of *The Field Afar* anything but absorbing.

She was somewhat aghast at what she had done but would say to herself, with a little thrill, *"This is the life I choose,"* and she had no intention of turning back! Sara became Sister M. Teresa and was in the first group professed at Maryknoll on February 15, 1921. She was an Assistant to Mother Mary Joseph during the formative years of the Maryknoll Sisters, and led the first group to Korea in 1924. She died peacefully at Bethany on March 13, 1957.

Mary Augustine Dwyer

In October 1911, the same day that Father Walsh accepted the applications of Mary Louise and Sara, he happened to go into the City and went to the office where Mary Augustine Dwyer was working. She was a clever, generous and complex woman and owned and managed a business office in Boston, often doing work *gratis* for Father. Being a public stenographer, she gave generously of time and materials in duplicating appeals for Fathers Walsh and Price, even sending them out for them.

When Father Walsh saw her in the office that day, he asked her if she would like to go to New York with the other two women. She said she would go, and made up a third in this trio of volunteers! The offers of these women seemed providential to Father Walsh who needed help for his new work. Mary Augustine brought to Hawthorne different office equipment which proved invaluable in their work. In 1913, she went to the newly-opened Venard in Scranton, PA, to assist with the bookkeeping and other tasks. In April 1916, Mary Augustine chose to leave and she re-established her former business in Boston.

Retreat at the Cenacle ~ January 1912

Mary Louise, Sara and Mary Augustine were strangers to each other, differed in age, training and disposition, and were bound by a common interest in foreign missions. A beginning experience of a five-day retreat at the Cenacle Convent on Riverside Drive in New York City, given by Mother Filippi, was arranged for them by Father Walsh. The retreat closed the morning of January 6, 1912, with a conference by Father Walsh, a talk which increased their sense of the importance of the undertaking and gave them practical advice for their new life.

Two Simple Agreements

On January 6, 1912, at the Cenacle in New York City before leaving for Hawthorne, the three Wise Women (Mary Louise Wholean, Sara Teresa Sullivan, Mary Augustine Dwyer) signed two simple agreements with Father Walsh:

> *1. We, the undersigned, receiving each from the Rev. James A. Walsh, a salary of $25 a month, with house-rent, kitchen service, light, telephone and heat free, hereby agree to merge our interests until July 1, 1912, sharing expenses, household and personal. These will be met from a common fund to be made up of the above money and any other monies that may come to any one or all of us in view of our union.*

2. *In consideration of $25 a month, for each as salary, and free rental, with light and heat, of a suitable house, we hereby agree to give to the Rev. James A. Walsh our services to be directed by him for the good of foreign missions. The agreement to hold until July 1, 1912.*

Arrival at Hawthorne
On the Feast of the Epiphany, January 6, 1912,
Mary Louise wrote in the diary:

We left New York for Hawthorne. 'Hawthorne, Hawthorne, Hawthorne,' shouted the conductor, and, looking out the window, we saw Father (Walsh) waiting for us. We walked through the little village until we came to a cottage perched on top of a snowy terrace. At the door we were welcomed by Father (John I.) Lane and a moment later, Father Price came to greet us.

Then we looked around ~ uncovered floors, bare table, cheerless rooms in which the furniture had been stacked, not arranged, and over all, the fading light of a cold, midwinter sun. I do not know what the others thought, but I know that I almost stopped thinking for a while and merely repeated over and over the words that Father had given us for a motto, 'For God and souls.' The motto worked its magic, however, and when some minutes later, I found myself making beds, however unskillfully, it had in some way sung itself into a joyful refrain.

The morning light did not improve the women's impression of the cottage which was so cold that they ate breakfast with their coats on and sat on the radiator in the evenings. The plumbing was primitive, reducing them to a quick splash from a basin half-filled with murky water. Sometimes there was no water for drinking, cooking or bathing ~ more than once they resorted to 'washing their hands' on the dew-covered grass. Yet, they rose every morning at six for a long day of work on *The Field Afar*, interspersed with prayers and manual labor.

Father Walsh tried to help. He hired a cook, a boy to unfreeze the pipelines and pump water, and a laundress willing to wash with almost no water. But their work was erratic and short-lived. The first cook departed, convinced the house was haunted. The group tried to maintain their enthusiasm. The glorious adventure for God did not feel so glorious after all.

The Secretaries

The women had to overcome many hardships to do all the clerical work involved in the publication of *The Field Afar*. They sent out circulars, did the literary work, as well as the bookkeeping and typing. The woman-helpers became known as the *secretaries,* a name covering many activities. In the early issues of *The Field Afar* in 1912 they were referred to by the all too poetic title, *'The Marys of Maryknoll.'*

The Name 'Maryknoll'

A few years earlier Father Walsh had coined the word, *Maryknoll*. He had vacationed in a beautiful resort in New Hampshire called *The Knolls*. This designation was combined with Father Price's profound devotion to Our Lady. Father Walsh told the secretaries:

> *Maryknoll will be the name of the knoll*
> *on which we shall locate permanently*
> *our seminary building.*

Mollie's First Visit to Hawthorne

For some years Mollie had offered all her free time to assist Father Walsh in the Boston Office for the Propagation of the Faith, and later at *The Field Afar* office. Father Walsh had spoken to his secretaries so often of Mollie's interest in the work and her untiring devotion to it that the women felt they already knew her. They knew she was prevented from joining them only by the fact that her assistance was necessary at home.

Mollie visited the secretaries on February 22, 1912, and stayed until the following Sunday. The diary account reads:

We had felt from the beginning that Mollie was one of us and so we were truly glad to have her with us for a few days. Of course, these days were happy ones. They could not be otherwise, brightened as they were by her merry good humor and sweetened by her constant self-forgetting helpfulness. We were so sorry to have her go as she was to leave us, and we resolved to pray with her that she might soon be able to come back and remain with us.

Mollie's visit had in truth uplifted the spirit of the secretaries!

Father Walsh's Hopes for Mollie

Although the women knew of Mollie's commitment to this foreign mission work from its inception, they now observed her willingness and ability to do any job that was needed. Her poise and self-assurance gave them a clearer sense of purpose and unity, characteristics that were also obvious to Father Walsh. If the group was to become a religious community ~ and he had written about that intention in *The Field Afar* as early as December 1911 ~ one among them would have to assume the leadership. For this, Father Walsh clearly pinned his hopes on Mollie.

From the beginning of their friendship in December 1906, Father Walsh had recognized Mollie's intelligence, her creativity, her generosity and her high ideals. He had shared with her his knowledge of the church's foreign missions, encouraged her in her spiritual journey and relied on her as his 'co-worker.' He prayed that she would join them soon in Hawthorne, and permanently.

A Reflective Moment

Realizing we are not the sole authors of our stories or our lives,
how has God's Spirit, often through others, influenced our lives?

Resources

The above Reflections were adapted from:
To the Uttermost Parts of the Earth
by Camilla Kennedy, MM;
Maryknoll's First Lady by Jeanne Marie Lyons, MM;
1912 *Teresian Diary;*
Hearts on Fire by Penny Lernoux;
Maryknoll in China by Jean-Paul Wiest;
On the Threshold of the Future
by Claudette LaVerdiere, MM;
Talk of Mother Mary Joseph ~ January 6, 1929,
and Archival Documents.

ဆာ   ဆာ   ဆာ

Mollie (on the right in the back row) at her home in
Jamaica Plain, MA, with her Mother on the left, and her
sisters, Louise (Sr. M. James) and Elizabeth in the front row.

#4 ~ Summer 1912

Mollie's Second Visit to Hawthorne, NY

In July 1912, Mollie arrived at Hawthorne and soon learned from Father Walsh: *"That it might be better for the secretaries to disband until a later date when the time might be ripe."* She came to know that the work of the women might have to be given up if she or someone like her did not appear.

With Father Walsh's assurance of continuing to give $25 a month to each of the secretaries, they were to be ready by September with a decision to remain or not to remain. Mollie joined the secretaries to help out during the summer in order to facilitate the decision-making process. The day-by-day experience of living with Mollie intangibly created an atmosphere that was unifying and personally freeing for the togetherness of Mary Louise, Sara, Mary Augustine and Nora. An excerpt from the 1912 Teresian Diary reads:

> *These were happy days with Mollie as generous, as resourceful, as organist and leading soprano, as cook, as shampooist, as gardener ~ she did every kind of work imaginable. Even the cat is so glad to be here that he has given up his wild ways, and rests contentedly in Mollie's lap.*

The personal presence of Mollie gifted each woman with the spirit of a natural born leader.

Mother Mary Alphonsa of Hawthorne

During the summer of 1912, Mollie came to know Mother Alphonsa, OP, the Founder of the Dominican Sisters of Hawthorne, who had befriended Father Walsh's women-helpers from the beginning. Born Rose Hawthorne, she was the third child of Nathaniel Hawthorne, the distinguished American novelist and short story writer.

With a keen sense of the social challenges of the new century, Mother Alphonsa had founded a community of Dominican Sisters in Hawthorne dedicated to the care of poor people who suffered from terminal cancer. This gentlewoman took a lively interest in the little community of "secretaries" who readily doubled as cooks and clerks, filling needs as they arose. Mother Alphonsa made their well-being her concern, especially when food and water were in short supply.

Mother Mary Alphonsa's Gift to Mollie

Inadvertently, it was Mother Alphonsa who would soon set the process in motion for Mollie's permanent return to Hawthorne. In July 1912, when Mollie came for a visit, she and Nora Shea walked over to meet Mother Alphonsa. From that first encounter until Mother Alphonsa's death on July 9, 1926, she and Mollie were close friends, despite the disparity in their ages. Mollie was not yet thirty and Mother Alphonsa was sixty-one when they met. Even before the two came to know each other well, Mollie's natural leadership was evident to Mother Alphonsa.

At their first meeting in 1912 she urged Mollie to stay with the group, so much did she want to see the women's work succeed. Mollie explained her financial obligations and family responsibilities and, half in jest, told Mother Alphonsa that if someone gave her two thousand dollars she would be able to stay. Mother Alphonsa went to see Father Walsh and told him that she had promised a thank-offering of $2,000 for a great favor her Community had received and she wanted to use it to make the women's part of the foreign mission work possible.

A few days later, on August 17, she urged Mollie: *"I want you to accept this gift, use it to meet those obligations and come back to Maryknoll this Fall!"* Only after Father Walsh and the secretaries had persuaded Mollie to accept the providential offer of the gift did Mollie make her decision. Mollie would join them in September. Time alone would reveal the importance of her decision to the future of the Maryknoll Sisters. On January 6, 1929, Mother Mary Joseph gave a talk to the Community, sharing that her family only used a small portion of the $2,000 gift, and they returned the rest for the work of Maryknoll. At the same talk she mused:

> *I have always felt that, if that particular incident had not come up, the work of our particular branch would not have gone on that year, and I am sure that, if the Community had broken up then, another beginning would never have been made.*

The Land Search

In July 1912, Father Walsh's first attempt to buy property from Mr. Joseph Oussani for his future seminary at nearby Pocantico Hills was effectively blocked by Mr. John D. Rockefeller, as he was bringing to completion his great stone mansion, Kykuit, and wanted to expand his property which was contiguous to this land. On August 14, 1912, Father Walsh, together with Monsignor John J. Dunn, Director of the Propagation of the Faith of New York, and Mollie, drove to Ossining to look over a second property for sale by a Mr. Law, a *"Hilltop Farm"* of ninety-three acres with four buildings:

1 - Two homesteads at a distance from each other: the larger one became the first Seminary and the other became St. Teresa's Lodge for the secretaries;

2 - A Carriage House, with quarters for hired help, became St. Michael's used as a Chapel for the Society, and later for the sisters' dormitories in the early 1920's;

3 - A Barn, that became St. Joseph's, was used by the Seminary students, and then in the early 1920's became the Sisters' Novitiate.

The Hilltop Farm immediately won their hearts: its woodland and fields, its height, its sweeping view of the magnificent Hudson River and the blue hills beyond. After a second visit Father Walsh decided, "This is Maryknoll!"

Mollie's Purchase of Ossining Property

On August 17, the very day Mollie received the generous gift from Mother Mary Alphonsa, another special event occurred which also involved her in Maryknoll's future: the purchase of a permanent piece of land for Maryknoll. In order to avert any possible prejudice toward a priest buyer, Mollie Rogers posed as a young woman buyer. Her chauffeur would be none other than Father James A. Walsh, well-disguised in linen duster and goggles. The sale was finalized within three hours in the afternoon of August 17, 1912, in White Plains, NY. It was an ordeal for Mollie, as Miss Rogers from Jamaica Plain, MA. Mollie commanded the situation as only she could, even to the point of keeping up her end of the conversation when Mr. Law indicated that she must be expecting a large family. Without hesitation Mollie said, *"Indeed, she was!"*

On the way back to Hawthorne, the car met the extra chauffeur, Father Walsh, who had been awaiting developments from afar. No one suspected that the long coat covered Father Walsh's clerical garb. A few days later Mollie legally transferred the property to the Catholic Foreign Mission Society of America for the price of one dollar.

The ending to such an event was a *Magnificat of Thanksgiving* ~ and Boston baked beans for supper! *Maryknoll moved onto the map!* Later when Mr. Law discovered that Miss Rogers had bought the land for the Maryknoll Society, he wrote a very gentlemanly letter in which he said that he welcomes Maryknoll and our influence.

Mollie in Jamaica Plain, MA

On August 21, Mollie left Hawthorne for a few weeks with her family in Jamaica Plain. Mollie wrote thanking Mother Alphonsa again for the generous gift saying:

> *I can do nothing in a material way to thank you - but so long as I live and for long after, if possible, at least a Memorare will be offered for you each day - a trifling thing in itself but powerful when laid at Our Lady's feet....My people have been most generous....and after the first passionate outbreak, unselfishly gave me up....Each one is striving to do all the little things they know I love, and we are all saying goodbye to the places that hold such dear memories of childhood. It is good to feel their love closing about me. My heart is a ragged old thing these days....Please pray for me.*

Mollie and Margaret Shea to Hawthorne

Mollie returned to Hawthorne on September 9, 1912, with Margaret Ann Shea, a young woman not yet eighteen. Margaret had come from nearby Melrose, MA, for an interview with Miss Rogers at her home on Robinwood Avenue, Jamaica Plain, telling Mollie that she wanted to help Father Walsh with his work for foreign missions. She related that she had called Father when he was in Boston recently to discuss the possibility, and he had referred her to a Miss Rogers, saying that whatever decision they reached together would be satisfactory to him. Margaret had been looking for a religious order. Until she found one that appealed to her, her confessor had suggested she volunteer to work in Father Walsh's foreign mission project. Margaret was wearing a long-sleeved black dress when she visited Mollie, making Mollie think that Margaret was a widow, but she looked too young to be that! They had a lovely visit and Mollie encouraged her: *"Let's just go together and see what God has in store for us!"* Margaret went with Mollie to Hawthorne and never turned back.

The group of secretaries now became six: Mary Louise Wholean, Sara Teresa Sullivan, Mary Augustine Dwyer, Nora Shea, Mollie and Margaret Shea! At this time Mollie was twenty-nine, and so was Mary Louise. Margaret was seventeen. The other three were all older than Mollie, Nora by only a few years, Sara was thirty-seven and Mary Dwyer was forty.

Leadership for the Secretaries

On September 14, a few days after Mollie and Margaret had arrived in Hawthorne, Father Walsh acted on his intention to place Mollie in charge. He wrote to Mary Louise, Sara, Mary Augustine and Nora asking:

Do you wish Mollie to direct you, that is, under my direction? Write me on this subject.... The diary notes: *Before the day was over we had all written to Father in reply to a note he had sent us this noon, and each had said 'yes.' Father was too busy to give us a conference, but sent us a note* (September 15), *in which he told us that Mary Joseph (Mollie) was to be head of the household until the Feast of the Epiphany, 1913.*

Though the reason is not clear, Father Walsh also bestowed on Mollie the more formal name of *Mary Joseph.* Although Mollie was only approaching her thirtieth birthday on October 27, she assumed her role as leader with grace. She never distanced herself from the group, whether she spoke with them about the spiritual life, restraint, punctuality, or a change in schedule. She maintained that a dignified spirit was required at all times, especially in view of the growing mixed population at Maryknoll. Moreover, she brought with her to Hawthorne the 'family spirit' and leadership abilities that had characterized so much of her youth and childhood.

Mollie's Accepting the Role of Directress

The secretaries found themselves moved deeply when Mollie expressed her appreciation of them and accepted her responsibility with these words:

I want you to know how wholly I belong to you in every hour of the day and night, to serve you, to love you, to watch over you and with you, under the guidance of the Holy Spirit, for of myself I can do nothing. Through Father Walsh and you I offer to this work the service of my entire being.

It was providential that just two years previously on September 15, 1910, Mollie had made a formal resolve to devote herself to mission work!

Mollie, Cook at the Seminary

On September 18, 1912, the Fathers, Students and Brothers moved from Hawthorne to *Maryknoll*, as Father Walsh was already calling his farm on the hill above Ossining. After a period of straightening up and settling down, which Father Walsh crisply defined as "chaos," and just as things were becoming normal, they woke up one morning to find that their cook had departed and left them breakfastless. Father Walsh had only to tell Mollie what had happened.

After consulting the secretaries, she set out immediately for Maryknoll from Hawthorne. Hannah, who had been cooking for the secretaries, joined Mollie the following day, and together they turned out three robust meals a day, with occasional evidence of Mollie's special touches. They also cleaned all the pots and pans, stocked the empty shelves, met the usual situations of unexpected guests, late and early dinners and the lack or delay of supplies.

Mollie and Hannah slept in the old farmhouse down the hill from the seminary ~ later St Teresa's Lodge. The farmer and his wife, Mr. & Mrs. Jenks, who still occupied it, offered each a room and a sagging bed. At the end of a long day Mollie would sink into hers too tired to stay awake and battle the cockroaches and bedbugs which came out in the dark.

One evening after the third meal of the day had been successfully turned out, Mollie went, tired and hot, to sit on the back steps of the Seminary and let the lovely evening air refresh her. She had not been sitting there long when a file of dark figures came around the corner of the house ~ Priests, Students and Brothers out for a short walk. The Fathers saw Mollie, lifted their hats and bowed their heads; the other young men tossed nods in her direction; and the well-fed line passed on down the hill. *"They had all had a very good supper, and a good dinner, and breakfast,"* Mollie thought. *"Why is it that we do not remember to say anything about food to the people who prepare it, unless there is something the matter with it?"* Not given to self-pity, she was as near discouragement as she could come.

Mollie went back to the kitchen, but she never forgot that people who create meals and others who help us deserve commendation just as much as artists, poets and philosophers ~ and perhaps even more!

A Glimpse of Margaret Ann Shea
(Who became our Sister M. Gemma)

Margaret was born on December 3, 1894, in Roxbury, MA. After high school, she worked as a dressmaker and then cared for children.

Margaret received the name Sister M. Gemma. Her first assignment as a Novice in 1920 was to work with the Japanese in Seattle, WA. Most of her mission life was working with the Japanese people. This was interrupted by the war in 1941 and she was interned with other religious women, and repatriated on the Gripsholm.

In 1949, she returned to Japan and spent the next 19 years there, before returning to Monrovia, and then to the Sisters Center, where she was an *Elder,* sharing generously the precious history of the early days. She died peacefully on January 8, 1993, just completing her 98th year.

A Reflective Moment

1 - How do the challenges, which our pioneers faced,
relate to those we face today?
2 - How is gratitude being nurtured in our lives?

Resources

The above Reflections were adapted from:
To the Uttermost Parts of the Earth by Camilla Kennedy, MM;
Maryknoll's First Lady by Jeanne Marie Lyons, MM;
1912 Teresian Diary;
On the Threshold of the Future by Claudette LaVerdiere, MM;
and Archival Documents.

80   80   80

#5 ~ The First Seven Secretaries

Front Row: Mary Louise Wholean, Anna Maria Towle, Mary Josephine Rogers,
Sara Sullivan. *Back Row:* Mary Augustine Dwyer, Nora Shea, Margaret Shea.

Move from Hawthorne to Maryknoll

On October 15, 1912, with the air of an Irish king bringing visiting royalty to his favorite castle, Maryknoll Brother Thomas McCann drove into the shaggy old Hilltop Farm in Ossining with the brand new name of *Maryknoll*. He made a royal gesture, welcoming them, *"Well, here we are!"* and then singing with his beautiful voice: *"Home, sweet home. Be it ever so humble!"* One after another the three secretaries climbed down stiffly from the carryall vehicle. Margaret Shea, red-cheeked, bundled in a house blanket and snuggling the cat; Mary Louise Wholean, gray with chill in spite of the carpets under which she and Anna Towle had hidden from the wind; Anna herself, a newcomer, with a beautiful youthful face, and striking white hair, carrying, of all things, an armful of summer hats!

Anna made straight for the Seminary kitchen, saying, *"Where's Mollie?"* Mollie came out, put her arms around each one of them and hurried them in to warm themselves by the kitchen stove. *"When the priests and boys are served,"* Mollie said, *"we will have our supper right here at the kitchen table together, as snug as you please. There will not be a stove in our house for a few days more at least."* These transplants from Hawthorne to Maryknoll felt that this inconsequential shift of personnel ~ three today, three more tomorrow ~ made up a really momentous occasion!

They knew that they were not coming to a well-prepared house. Mr. and Mrs. Jenks and their family had just vacated it the day before. Part of their furniture, awaiting a moving van, still clogged the lower rooms and hallway. Carpenters and plumbers were already at work making repairs and a lot of dirt!

Mollie, with her position as head cook at the Seminary, had no time to work any transformation in this hodgepodge. To commemorate the day of their coming and to honor the great Carmelite whose feast it was, Father Walsh had already christened the old house 'St. Teresa's.' Then Mollie opened the door, went ahead into the darkness and lit a kerosene lamp, and the other three followed her into the house, knowing they were home.

Arrival of Sara Teresa Sullivan, Mary Augustine Dwyer and Nora Shea

In the afternoon of October 16, Sara, Mary Augustine and Nora arrived. They had a tour of their new home from the first floor to the third. It was an old-fashioned building with twenty-two mostly small rooms. The long room at the front would be used as an office for *The Field Afar* magazine. Back of this was a large hall, then the community room, dining room and kitchen. Also on the first floor were two small rooms that could serve eventually as a chapel. With the rusted pipes, loosening plaster, rough floor boards and leaking roof, the old lodge challenged Mollie's homemaking and ingenuity, and taxed Father Walsh's feeble finances to bring it into repair.

Making St. Teresa's Lodge a Home

The Teresian Diary gives a good picture of the days
following the move from Hawthorne, as Mary Louise writes:

We are still camping out in the Seminary kitchen for our meals. We piece out the number of chairs by using boxes and making a bench out of the ironing board, and we manage to make three knives and forks do service for eight people (includes cook), each one sharing with her neighbors and, in case of emergency, appropriating the potato knife and toasting fork.

Mary Joseph returned to us on October 17, having been relieved of her duties in the Seminary kitchen by the arrival of a new cook, an aspirant Brother. We are still living with trunks packed and bureaus locked. We worked under difficulties with no light, and no heat. The cistern is now full of water and the water is full of worms.

Mary Joseph and Margaret continued the settling process of laying rugs, placing furniture, hanging pictures, and painting the altar between times. We welcomed with joy the advent of heat in our radiators, real heat which drove away the shivers that have been chasing each other up and down our spinal columns for weeks.

Reminiscing in 1931, Mother Mary Joseph exclaimed:

Fifty minutes from Broadway we were! But there were only oil lamps those days to make bright the rambling, decrepit, old house, and swinging lanterns to light the paths to the chicken house and barn. But Mother liked those days, describing them as idyllic; our lives pastoral. Our father seldom had two coins to jingle in his pocket, the houses were only an hour from Broadway, and were devoid of the most ordinary conveniences, and we literally lived from one day to another. But we were profoundly happy and at peace.

The old house had charm and character,
and Mollie gave herself cheerfully to making the most of its good points.
She loved it most of all because it was "*the cradle of a great hope.*"

The Teresians of Maryknoll

After the secretaries were settled at St. Teresa's Lodge, Mill Hill Father McCabe, who had been teaching at the Maryknoll Seminary, sent a postcard from England to them. He addressed it to '*The Teresians.*' The name took hold immediately and the secretaries, already dedicated to St. Teresa of Avila, became '*The Teresians of Maryknoll.*'

Maryknoll's First Christmas Eve 1912

Mother Mary Joseph in her sharing with the Novices,
January 2, 1947, tells the story of the first Christmas Eve
at Maryknoll in 1912:

The snow was still falling on a hillside already so thickly blanketed that no familiar landmarks were in sight. Father Walsh with Bradford, 'our boy of all work,' appeared at St. Teresa's Lodge with horse and sleigh and I was asked to go to Ossining to advise Father on his Christmas shopping. I sat in the sleigh, while Father looked things over in the stores. Bradford brought out the presents for inspection. There was a gift for each of the secretaries which had to be wrapped later.

Father Walsh apparently did not think it was proper for Mollie to go into the store with him, so she sat patiently outside in the open sleigh in the freezing weather!

Christmas 1912

Mary Louise notes in the Teresian Diary:

The first Christmas at Maryknoll began with a Midnight Mass sung by Father Price with Father Walsh playing the organ. As we walked over to the Seminary, our path was lighted by the clear brightness of a full moon and stars that sparkled with joyful radiance. The spirit of Christmas was in the air and when later Christ was really born again in the hands of the priest and in our own souls, it all seemed quite as wonderful as if we had been present at the Savior's coming in Bethlehem nineteen hundred years ago. At sunrise we had two Masses here. Father Walsh said them both and for the first one we sang three hymns, Holy Night, Adeste Fideles and Judea's Sacred, Silent Hills.

After the second Mass, Father had his breakfast in the room next to the chapel that we had arranged as a sacristy, and we went to the dining room for our feast ~ properly so-called because we had grapefruit! We were filled with the thoughts that Father suggested to us at Mass, a deep gratitude that we were allowed to be here, and a keen appreciation of his privilege and ours. After breakfast, Father Walsh came out to wish us each a Merry Christmas and not long after, Father (John I.) Lane and Father McCabe telephoned their greetings.

The secretaries had a delicious Christmas dinner together, with surprise cards that Sara and Mary Augustine had made. After dinner, Mary Joseph and Nora left for their allotted days at home. Bradford drove them to the train and Mary Augustine rode with them. *"They were waved away from the house with brooms and feather dusters, and at the Seminary gate they were bombarded with snowballs by the students who were having a snow frolic!"*

Mary Joseph Again Accepted as Directress

We each signed and gave to Father Walsh this Sunday morning, January 19, 1913, the following form: *"I am willing to acknowledge Mary Josephine Rogers as our Directress at St. Teresa's Lodge, until January 6, 1914, and I promise to do my best to assist her, realizing that community life demands self-surrender for the glory of God, for the salvation of souls, and for my own spiritual progress."* Father prefaced his conference by a few words on our acceptance of Mary Joseph as our Directress, urging us to help her and to relieve her in every way possible, and assuring us of love and devotion on her part towards us.

A Uniform Dress for the Teresians
The Teresian Diary for February 6, 1913:

Mary Joseph dressed up in her 'habit' which Anna is making. We were all delighted with it and Father pronounced it good. The material is gray gingham, with a white collar and cuffs. The skirt and waist have pleats for fullness, and there is a cape or circular collar extending over the shoulders. Around the waist there is to be a cincture of heavier material than the dress. At the end of this, the Chi Rho is to be embroidered in blue, and at the neck we are to wear the medal of Blessed Theophane Venard.

Anna finished Mary Joseph's "habit" and began the others. When all the Teresians put on their new gray uniforms, Brother Thomas was nearly prostrated at the sight of the *'old ladies in gray'* and Father Walsh remarked that he was strongly reminded of his visit to Sherburne Women's Prison, not many miles outside Boston!

Name: Maryknoll ~ One Family
Father Walsh had used the name *Maryknoll* on his stationery since his arrival at Hawthorne. In the 1912 October/November issues of *The Field Afar* he announced the new site and bestowed on it the permanent name of *Maryknoll*. In his report to Rome at the end of the first year, Father Walsh discreetly described his growing missionary community:

Towards the end of September we opened with six students, two for Theology and four for Philosophy. We have also with us three aspirant Brothers, and, in a private house at one corner of our grounds, and shortly to be enclosed, is a group of seven faithful women, who are serving the cause by clerical and domestic assistance. Four of these have been aiding the work from the beginning. They are lay-women who would gladly welcome the religious life, and who are practically leading such, as is evidenced by their daily Communion, rule of silence, and willingness to give their labor to the Church without any material compensation.

Thus, from the beginning of Maryknoll there existed three branches ~ the priests, the brothers, and the women who longed to be religious. Each branch came from the same tree, and each depended upon the others for its growth and mutual support. All shared the same Founders with their ideals, aspirations and spiritual motivation, growing together as one family with a common history and identity.

Just A Postscript
Sister Anna Maria Towle, MM

Anna Maria was born in Ireland, and was 48 years old when she joined the women-helpers, becoming the seventh member of the community. She arrived first at Maryknoll in Ossining, NY, on October 4, 1912, where Mollie was overseeing the Seminary kitchen.

Then on October 6, Mollie brought Anna to Hawthorne where she stayed with the secretaries till they moved to Maryknoll in Ossining. Anna brought with her a seemingly infinite capacity for work, and her special talent was sewing.

When Sister Anna Maria died on February 4, 1944, Maryknoll Father John Considine said she possessed the *"sacrament of the present moment"* ~ living in a perpetual now, as if she seemed to say: *"If someone comes to me now, I give myself completely to them now for they need me now!"* Her life became a perpetual now bridging eternity. She lived calmly, happily in this continual now, till she passed gracefully into the eternal now!

A Reflective Moment
How does the spirit of the first seven
Teresians grace our lives today?

Resources
The above Reflections were adapted from:
To the Uttermost Parts of the Earth
by Camilla Kennedy, MM;
Maryknoll's First Lady by Jeanne Marie Lyons, MM;
1912-1913 Teresian Diary;
Mother Mary Joseph's Talk to Novices, 1947;
On the Threshold of the Future
by Claudette LaVerdiere, MM;
The Spirituality of Mollie Rogers
by Elizabeth E. Carr, Ph.D.;
and Archival Documents.

80   80   80

Mollie feeding the calves.

#6 ~ Some Events at Maryknoll in 1913

Teresians' Future as Religious Community

The question of the Teresians' future as a religious community was a regular topic of discussion, as noted in the *Teresian Diary*. Mary Louise Wholean's entry on June 5, 1912, mentions that Father James A. Walsh had spoken about it with her that morning. Religious life was uncharted territory for the women. Few, if any of them, had known religious sisters or had ever had any opportunity to observe them firsthand. For this reason they relied heavily on Father Walsh for direction and assistance.

Almost as soon as the women arrived, he suggested a daily timetable that would ensure the primacy of prayer in their lives. He also gave frequent conferences to nourish them spiritually. He regretted that he could do little, especially in the first year, to assist them in organizing their new community. However, the future of the secretaries remained uppermost among the many concerns that absorbed his energies.

Father Borgmann's Retreat

In January 1913, the Teresians celebrated their first anniversary at Maryknoll with a retreat led by Father Henry Borgmann, a Redemptorist priest. They entered into this graced time with a clear ongoing desire for the vowed life. The women felt there might not be a future at all unless they formed a permanent organization. Father Borgmann led the group to a more profound understanding of the spirituality that would sustain them throughout this period. He spoke of Teresa of Avila, the model and patron Father Walsh had given them, emphasizing her thorough and down-to-earth approach to God. He further challenged the women with his favorite maxim, '*Know yourself; know God.*' He urged them to use the Missal, which was not the common custom of that era. This retreat was Mary Joseph's first such experience.

Despite the fact that the women had to continue with some of their work, she was totally caught up in the conferences and prayers. Each one savored the time for reflection that strengthened their resolve to dedicate their lives to the work of foreign missions.

The Death of Mollie's Father

On March 4, 1913, Mary Joseph received a message from Jamaica Plain that her father had collapsed, was paralyzed and unable to speak. She immediately traveled to Boston and remained at his bedside for two months. He died on May first, and a week later Mary Joseph returned to Maryknoll, welcomed with a *"chorus of joyful shouts"* by the Teresians. Father Walsh came over after supper and they all had a beautiful evening sharing together.

A Red-Letter Day with the "Redness" Left Out

After breakfast on May 5, Father Walsh told the Teresians that Cardinal Farley was coming to visit Maryknoll in the afternoon. He asked them to put on their uniforms, which had been hanging in the closets. So the hustle and bustle began. They gave everything an extra sweep and a special flourish of the duster. Sara hung some pictures in the office. Anna put the last stitches in her uniform and covered a cushion with red satin on one side only, because the remnant was a small one. They took turns at pressing their dresses and after a hasty attempt at dinner, hurried upstairs to put them on. The afternoon went on with nothing more exciting than the noise of the hammer as two of the students put on some stray door knobs.

Then, about four o'clock, there was a loud crash and, following the direction of the noise to the community room, they discovered that the ceiling was resting in pieces on the floor, table and chairs. The debris was shoveled out and once more they worked and waited. However, the Cardinal did not come! The anticipation of his visit had, however, accomplished something. They had put on their uniforms and they had several repairs made about the house!

Feast of St. Peter and St. Paul

The Teresian Diary relates:

June 29, 1913, Feast of St. Peter and St. Paul, Father Walsh sang High Mass and Mary Joseph played the organ. Father spoke of the significance of the day, marking the end of the scholastic year and the second milestone in the history of the Society. In the afternoon at six o'clock Father came to give us our cinctures, postponed from the 24th of May. In his conference Father spoke of the significance of our putting on the cinctures with the Chi Rho within a circle, which is a symbol of Christ's worldwide mission.

The Venard in Scranton, PA
On July 1, 1913, Father Walsh sent the following letter
to Mary Joseph and the Teresians:

We will need at Scranton a woman to assist Father John I. Lane: 1) As supervising housekeeper, 2) As secretary and accountant. We have decided that, although our numbers are few at Maryknoll, one of our own should be at Scranton. I do not wish to ask any one of you to go, but I do ask for volunteers. Please read this note to all your flock, instruct them not to act hastily, but to say a prayer and leave a note in my basket before next Monday.

On July 31, Father Walsh returned from a long trip. After supper on August first, he visited the Teresians, giving an interesting account of his trip, including his visits to Detroit, Notre Dame in Indiana, Chicago, Des Moines, St. Louis and Scranton, where he encountered difficulty in leasing a house for the Apostolic School.

Finally came the announcement that Mary Augustine Dwyer was chosen to go to Scranton. Father Walsh said he considered the position a very responsible one, a possible beginning of a series of foundations of the same kind. On September 8, Mary Augustine left for the Venard.

Miss Julia Ward
The Teresian Diary relates:

We were delighted to see our Fairy Princess, Julia Ward. After inspecting our house from attic to cellar, she promised all kinds of improvements: new floors and ceilings, wall paper, a closet for each bedroom, rugs, a well-lighted sewing room for Anna and a 'sanitary' kitchen.

She even feared that our uniforms would not be warm enough for the winter and offered to get heavier material and send up two or three women to make the dresses for us. She also took upon herself the duty of providing winter cloaks and hats. She asked Mary Joseph to write to her at any time for whatever we might need. The story of these wonders, as Mary Joseph told it to us, sounded like a midsummer night's dream, but the best part of it was that we knew it to be true.

Also, in September-October 1913, a Chapel was added to the Society Farm-house Seminary and Julia paid for all the furnishings for the new Chapel. Father Walsh called Miss Julia Ward ~ 'Lady Bountiful!'

St. Teresa's Day 1913

October 15, the great St. Teresa's Day, we had enjoyed pretending that we were going to sleep late, but of course we got up at the usual time. Father Walsh said Mass for us. When we came into the dining room, we found the first surprise. The room was hung with strips of yellow and white crepe paper, and the pictures were decorated with autumn leaves. On the table were eight St. Teresa dolls dressed in a Carmelite habit of brown and white crepe paper. Anna Maria Towle had made them and not even the cincture of white knotted string was left out.

After breakfast we dressed up the dog and cat with bows of crepe paper, so that the whole family might have a share in the festivities. A remembrance we much appreciated was a bouquet of carnations from the students. Later a box of candy came from Father Walsh, and Mrs. Grant and her daughter sent us some hot doughnuts and a cake. At dinner we had ice cream. At six o'clock Father gave us a talk on St. Teresa. He told us it was especially fitting that we take St. Teresa as our patron. He mentioned the importance of our work and showed how necessary our services were for the advancement of the Seminary at this time. After supper, the students came over to see the decorations. As soon as they left, we started a combined concert and dance, to the accompaniment of popular music played on the organ. A good bit of merriment ended the celebration of our great holiday!

Some Additional News from the 1913 Teresian Diary

➢ *Among the guests were Father Walsh's sister, Mrs. Hughes, who spent a few days with us. Our guests were a bit frightened by the prospect of falling ceilings, at any time and in any place, and wondered if they would ever survive the cold and other inconveniences.*

➢ *Father John I. Lane wrote Father Walsh that Mary Augustine was "panning out beautifully at the Venard doing all kinds of things well."*

➢ *Father Price asked the Teresians to call him Father Bernadette. He blessed the statues of Our Lady of Lourdes he had given them, touching them with a bit of rock cut from the spot where the Blessed Virgin stood.*

➢ *The Teresians had a triduum, praying to St. Luke for funds, and the receipts amounted to more than $200. They then began a Novena to St. Philomena for the same purpose!*

> ➤ *On October 30, we went to the Seminary for the blessing of the bell. The ceremony was performed by Monsignor Edwards, who was in charge of all the Religious Sisters in the Archdiocese of NY. The Bell was named "Paul," and Father Walsh and Mary Joseph were the sponsors. The service was impressive, in spite of the fact that we wanted to laugh when the sponsors hit the bell with a piece of wood for lack of anything better at hand!*

Present Mission Departure Bell

We learned from the Archives that the 1913 Bell is not the present Mission Departure Bell in the Society's Quadrangle. Father James A. Walsh made a trip to Asia in 1917-1918 and on his way home he stopped in Japan and received a gift of a Bell from a resident missioner, Father Defrennes of Fukushima. The Bell was from a Japanese Temple that had burned in Sendai. Father Defrennes arranged to have the 200-pound Bell taken to Yokohama from where Father Walsh was departing. Father Walsh and the Bell arrived in New York in April, 1918, and the Bell was used in the Society's first Departure Ceremony on September 7, 1918.

A Reflective Moment

Sorrow, disappointments, calamities, change
and joys weaved through the lives of the
Teresians. How are these realities embraced
in our lives today?

Resources

The above Reflections were adapted from:
Maryknoll's First Lady by Jeanne Marie Lyons, MM;
The 1913 Teresian Diary,
On the Threshold of the Future
by Claudette LaVerdiere, MM;
and Archival Material.

ଓ ଓ ଓ

#7 ~ The Field Afar ~ Its Beginnings

The quote on either side of the *Chi Rho* said in Latin and English:
"To those who love God, all things work together for good" (Romans 8:28).

Mollie's Mission Study Club

Mollie's decision to organize a Catholic Mission Study Club at Smith College in 1906 turned out to be one of the most important gifts in her life and the lives of the Maryknoll Sisters. Because of the lack of any Catholic materials on this subject, she wrote in October 1906, at the suggestion of a priest in her parish, to Father James A. Walsh, Boston's Society of the Propagation of the Faith (SPF) Director. The letter revealed that the particular motive of these classes was to invite young women to do actual mission work when they leave college. Her plan had four objectives: the preparation needed for priests and nuns for mission work; the mission orders and their field of work; the type of work; and the collection and distribution of funds for the missions. Mollie asked for information *in English, French or Latin,* ending prophetically, *"who knows but that the little work we do here may be the beginning of greater efforts in later life."* Father Walsh responded quickly, suggesting that Mollie include in her study plan *"the martyr spirit of our age,"* and he invited her to visit him.

Mollie's Initiation to "The Field Afar"

During the 1906 Christmas holidays, Mollie had her first visit with Father Walsh. On his desk were the galley proofs of the first issue of *The Field Afar,* a bimonthly publication beginning January 1, 1907. He spread them out, giving her a lesson in paging, correction-making and telling her the genesis of this project. The aim of *The Field Afar* was forthrightly stated on its editorial page: *"To deepen and widen in its readers the missionary spirit."*

That winter of 1906 and the following spring when not at her duties at Smith College, Mollie gave her free time to what she already had accepted as a great cause. She translated French letters and articles that were used in *The Field Afar.*

Father Walsh printed Mollie's October 1906 letter in the May 1907 editorial of *The Field Afar* for the *edification of the readers.* Also, he was so pleased with the program Mollie planned and carried out for the students at Smith College that he presented it in *The Field Afar* issues, October 1907 and February 1908, as a model and incentive for other study groups.

During vacation time in 1907, Mollie went every day to the SPF Office in Boston, where Father Walsh squeezed in another desk and called it hers. She translated, edited, composed articles and removed heavy cardboard from pictures to be filed, which she took home and put to soak in the bathtub, with overwhelming tolerance of her family! From 1908 until 1911, Mollie gave all her spare time to work with Father Walsh. His gratitude was evidenced by a Christmas gift she received from him on December 24, 1908 ~ a bound copy of the first year's issues of *The Field Afar*. On the flyleaf Father Walsh had written in his swinging script, *"To my co-worker with deep appreciation of her faithful service."* It remained one of the few treasures which Mollie kept and brought with her when she left her home for Hawthorne, NY, nearly four years later.

Archbishops' Approval of The Catholic Foreign Mission Society of America (CFMSA)

On April 27, 1911, the Archbishops met at the Catholic University of America in Washington, DC, to discuss a proposal for a CFMSA. Father Price waited outside the Conference Room, while Father Walsh worked at his desk in the SPF Office in Boston, trying to keep his mind on what he was doing. Nora at her typewriter, and Mollie in her classroom, also had this one preoccupation filling the whole background of their consciousness. In the late afternoon, Father Walsh joyfully told Nora: *"Miss Shea, the word has come. Unanimously approved!"*

Mollie, returning home from school, heard the wonderful news! That evening it was in the late papers. Things moved quickly after that.

Moving The Field Afar Office

Father Walsh was released from his duties as the Society of the Propagation of the Faith Director. *The Field Afar* now needed new quarters. The Washington Press in Jamaica Plain, which printed *The Field Afar,* offered Father space in their plant. The space consisted of a long storeroom, small and stuffy, unbelievably dirty at the moment and permanently subject to the noise of the printing presses thumping, clanging and grating just the other side of the thin wall!

Mollie and Nora went to work with brooms, wall brushes and scrub brushes. They were stiff and groaning but still good-natured by the time they were finished. They arranged the two desks and the empty file cases into the semblance of an office and learned to shout at each other at the top of their voices over the noise of the presses.

Writing New Index Cards for The Field Afar

The Field Afar subscription list of over 7,000 names and the SPF patrons had all been entered on the same index cards. These cards were needed in the SPF office during the day. Mollie offered to bring the files home, drawer by drawer, at five o'clock each day and bring them back before nine the next morning, riding the public transportation from Boston to Jamaica Plain.

After supper, Mollie, her parents, siblings and friends sat around the big dining room table and copied the names and subscription information of *The Field Afar* subscribers on new index cards. Mollie's Mother would bring the night's task to a close with some treat as their reward. Years later at Maryknoll, Mollie would come across an index card written in her mother's or father's hand and it would bring back precious memories of her family's sharing in the beginning days of Maryknoll!

Rome's Approval of the CFMSA

At the end of May, Father Walsh appointed Mollie to be in charge of the editorial work of *The Field Afar* and Nora Shea, the administrative work, when he and Father Price left for Rome.

On June 29, 1911, the Feast of Sts. Peter and Paul, Fathers Walsh and Price were in Rome and received the word from Cardinal Gotti that their plan for the CFMSA had been approved by Pope Pius X. Back in Boston, Mollie and Nora were overjoyed. During the long hot summer, Mollie and Nora had worked away on *The Field Afar*. How much Father Walsh relied on Mollie could be judged from a cable which he sent to the Washington Press that July: *Print FA. Rogers fill space.* This he followed up with a letter to Mollie, saying, *"I know that you have used good judgment."*

Hawthorne, New York ~ First Site for Mission Society

On September 19, 1911, Fathers Walsh and Price were back in Boston. A decision had been reached to locate the Seminary-to-be and *The Field Afar* office in the New York Archdiocese. In October, Fathers Walsh and Price accepted the hospitality from the French Dominican Fathers at Hawthorne.

The Field Afar Magazine and the Secretaries

Father Walsh rented two rooms at Hood House (Warren Avenue in Hawthorne) for *The Field Afar* office. Tulph Cottage on Marietta Avenue was rented for the three new secretaries: Mary Louise Wholean, Sara Sullivan and Mary Dwyer, who arrived on January 6, 1912. They worked daily on *The Field Afar* magazine, walking to and from their house to Hood House on Warren Avenue. Their days and nights were dedicated to *The Field Afar*. In April 1912, they moved to Rau House on Linda Avenue, which was large enough to accommodate both home and work space. The front room was transformed into *The Field Afar* office.

Mary Louise, an exact and careful worker with a fine-honed mind and a good grasp of languages, helped with the editorial work, giving attention particularly to missionary articles and letters contributed from the field, many of them in French, some in Italian and German. These she translated and edited. She was to prepare occasional articles for the daily press and mission notes for the Providence, RI, *Visitor* and the Hartford, CT, *Transcript*. And like the other two secretaries, she was to help wrap and mail *The Field Afar,* which now had a circulation of about 10,000 subscribers. Mary Dwyer was the bookkeeper, took dictation, did the multigraphing, had charge of stock and was responsible for all the ordering and shipping.

Sara Sullivan was responsible for the bulky and antiquated addressograph which printed the monthly wrappers for *The Field Afar*. She had charge of the subscribers' index cards and stencils, sent acknowledgments to new subscribers and urged the lapsed to renew their subscriptions. Nora Shea often came from Boston for temporary stays to help the secretaries, helping wherever she was most needed. On April 17, 1912, she came to stay.

Mollie did not let anyone at home guess what she felt about these new developments. She did not abandon the hope of someday being a volunteer in Father Walsh's little group, but her family needed her. Her hope was realized on September 9, 1912, when she and Margaret Shea arrived at Hawthorne.

The Teresian Diary includes much information regarding the strenuous work involved in producing *The Field Afar* magazine. We share a few excerpts from the 1912 Diary:

The Field Afar arrived and we all set to work folding the papers in their envelopes and getting them ready for mailing. Our one-time dining room resembles a first-class post office. Every available space is covered with envelopes. Woe to anyone who puts Michigan on the Minnesota chair, or knocks over the State of Connecticut, which rises above the table like The Leaning Tower of Pisa.

The Last Field Afar Issue Sent from Hawthorne

We worked quite calmly until 4:30, when Father appeared with a determination to rush off The Field Afar material so that the last issue could be sent out from the Hawthorne Post Office before the move to Ossining. In about three minutes we were spinning around like pinwheels, each one trying to catch up with herself and with the particular task that had fallen to her lot. The office sounded like a full-sized machine shop, with Mary Augustine turning the crank of the multigraph and Sara running the addressograph. We are struggling day and night to keep our heads above The Field Afar, which is pouring in upon us in bundles of ever-increasing size!

Father Walsh writes in jest and in truth
in *The Field Afar* July 1916 issue:

Unfortunately for us, the Teresians have learned that we cannot get along without them, unless we wish to give up The Field Afar and that would be suicide!

Through their translating, editing and clerical work, the Teresians maintained *The Field Afar,* which Father Walsh called **'Maryknoll's Lifeline!'** *The Field Afar* was the conduit for the Catholic Foreign Mission Society of America's vocations and monetary gifts.

A Reflective Moment

Like Mollie and the other Teresians, how are our faith,
trust and sense of mission growing wherever we are ?

Resources

The above Reflections were adapted from:
Maryknoll's First *Lady* by Jeanne Marie Lyons, MM;
1912 Teresian Diary;
Maryknoll in China by Jean-Paul Wiest.

ဢ ဢ ဢ

#8 ~ The Field Afar Blossoms

Mother Mary Joseph and Sister Marie Pierre Semler
preparing pictures for *The Field Afar* in 1925.

The arrival of *The Field Afar (FA)* for mailing always brought strenuous work for all the Teresians. The wrapping was done at St. Teresa's Lodge until *The Field Afar* building was built in 1915. Each issue had to be hand-wrapped, the paste of a consistency that would flow but not soak the paper. There was a special technique to yanking the top wrapper from under the paste pot and, with a flip of the wrist, rolling the magazine inside the wrapper to show the address. The Teresians could remember when a dozen of them in 1917 took days to wrap and mail *The FA's* 35,000 copies. They were amazed to discover that in 1923, with their increase in personnel and circulation of over 100,000, they could, and did, wrap up to 22,000 FA's in two-hours!

The announcement in the June 1918 issue of *The FA* that Maryknoll found a mission field in China signaled a new growth for the magazine. When reports of the first Maryknollers in Yeungkong appeared six months later, about a thousand new subscribers joined monthly. During the Depression Years circulation fell below 100,000, but then rebounded, and by 1939 there was a circulation of 216,000. By 1949, when Maryknollers were expelled from China, there were over 600,000 subscribers.

Mollie's Gifts and The Field Afar

Mollie found herself unusually gifted with a great ability to express her thoughts spontaneously in the written word. Her early years of editorial work on *The Field Afar* served the purpose of mission well as her skill took the basic forms of mission communication in letters, diary accounts of travel and spiritual conferences.

In 1913, a collection of mostly fictitious short stories was published under the title *Stories From The Field Afar*. About two-thirds of the fifteen stories were written by Mollie Rogers, and one-third by Father Walsh, all under the pseudonym, John Wakefield. Each account dealt with an aspect of mission life in China.

An entry in the 1913 Teresian Diary related that in the midst of their work: *"The first Maryknoll chickens pecked their way through their shells and were immediately given a bed in a Field Afar envelope box (being too cold outside), that they might realize from the start that they were missionary chickens."*

Father Chin

The Field Afar chose special audiences among the subscribers. One important group was school children. In the first issue, 1907, Father John I. Lane started *Our Young Apostles,* a column under the pen name of Father Ignatius, which dealt almost exclusively with China. Father Lane's precarious health and new responsibilities forced him to give up the column in 1912. In March 1916, Father Ignatius' column reappeared as a four-page supplement called *The Maryknoll Junior.* Father Chin was introduced to the readers: *"He has spent a portion of his life in China and if he had stayed there longer, he would be called Father China!"*

Father Chin became so successful that in April of 1919 *The Maryknoll Junior* became an independent magazine, which reached 15,000 young subscribers by 1924. The articles of Father Chin were written by different sisters, including Sister M. Theodore Farley.

Catholic Mission Crusade

When the Society of the Divine Word launched the Catholic Students' Mission Crusade in 1917, *The Field Afar* gave enthusiastic support. Starting with the first national convention in Techny, Illinois, in July 1918, Maryknollers always attended meetings of the Mission Crusade. Mother Mary Joseph, Fathers Raymond Lane and James Drought addressed the students at the 7th National Convention in 1931.

Father James A. Walsh was a guest speaker at the meeting in 1933. Both Mother Mary Joseph's and Father Walsh's talks relied heavily on examples from the Maryknoll experience in China.

Father John Considine and The Field Afar

In January 1937, Father John Considine, Editor of *The Field Afar,* organized the Maryknoll Mission Education Bureau. Gathering Maryknollers, especially sisters with literary, dramatic or artistic talents, he divided the Bureau into five sections: *Press, Reference and Research Services, Entertainment, Lectures* and *Schools.* The first two books prepared under the aegis of the Education Bureau were written by Father Considine and Sister Alma Erhard, who was in charge of the School Section.

Following in the footsteps of Father Considine and Sister Alma, Maryknollers wrote about 50 books on foreign missions between 1940 and 1955. As early as 1929, Maryknoll made a weekly appearance on the Paulist Radio Station WLWL in New York City. This was the beginning of several Maryknoll radio shows of which *Father Chin's Chats* of the mid-1950's were the most popular.

Maryknoll Sisters and Reaching the Young

During the 1930's, prior to establishing the Mission Education Bureau, the Maryknoll Sisters were responsible for the only organized Maryknoll effort to reach young people. As head of what was then known as Mission Education Activities, Sister Alma Erhard had gathered a team of enterprising and creative sisters who edited *The Maryknoll Junior* and most of the literature appealing to youth.

Sister Immaculata Brennan was Sister Alma's Associate Director. She had a special talent for writing and editing school plays and was later responsible for plays in the entertainment and lecture section of Father Considine's Education Bureau. Less than a year after the official opening of the Bureau, she had prepared some 25 plays that included directions for staging, costuming and music.

Sister Immaculata Brennan's plays were written for each part of the liturgical year and accommodated all age groups from primary school children to college students and adults, for an all-male or all-female cast.

The School Section

The task of the fifth division of the Mission Education Bureau, the School Section, was to provide teaching materials which would "*build mission ideals in the hearts of the young people of school age.*" Father Considine entrusted the entire direction of the School Section to Sister Alma and her team. The group compromised a wide range of talented Maryknoll Sisters.

An accomplished author, Sister Alma wrote extensively for *The Field Afar, The Maryknoll Junior,* the Play Library and the Maryknoll Bookshelf under a variety of pseudonyms, ranging from *S.M.A.* and *Marie Fisher* to more exotic names such as *Autumn Fairy* or *Granma Li Li.* Sister Chaminade Dreisoerner, who edited the materials, became indispensable as the number of school-oriented publications increased.

Sister Louise (Maria Giovanni) Trevisan, a professional illustrator, brought the books alive with her drawings and paintings. In the early 1950's, she also developed several series of popular teaching cards on the Mass, the Sacraments and various Mission Countries.

As the years went by, several sister-writers were added to Sister Alma's team; including the especially talented Sister Juliana Bedier, a veteran of 12 years in the Far East, who began writing in 1937. By the mid-1950's, she had written or co-authored 28 books, 24 filmstrips and countless articles, mostly for children of kindergarten and primary-school age.

In October 1938, Sister Juliana, together with Father John Considine, Sisters Alma Erhard and Grace Martel, launched *Mission Time*. This bi-monthly bulletin was published during the school year to provide Catholic teachers with guidance and inspiration on how to inculcate mission ideals in their students. Each issue offered a mine of information on the missions, as well as lesson plans to give the teachers a missionary dimension to their various classes.

Sister Juliana also prepared a three-volume series on teaching religion in the classroom, entitled *Religion Teacher and the World*. She was the main driving force behind *The Catholic Geography Series* published by William H. Sadlier for grammar school children. Between 1948 and 1952, she wrote three volumes and co-authored the others in this nine-volume series. The Geography Series was widely adopted and appreciated in Catholic schools throughout the United States. From 1945 to 1947, Sister Juliana's efforts were continued at the high school level by Sister Mary Just David.

Influence of The Field Afar

The Field Afar was undoubtedly the major attraction to Maryknoll. In *The Secret of Maryknoll,* an article published in the October 1950 issue of the magazine, the editor wrote: *"Every year we make a survey of our new students to determine the sources of their vocations. Over 60 percent of them were introduced to Maryknoll by The Field Afar."*

The Maryknoll Sisters continued to carry on the legacy of their Teresian days by performing most of the housekeeping tasks at the Major Seminary at Maryknoll, NY, and the Venard Preparatory Seminary in Scranton, PA. They did the cooking, canning, cleaning, laundry, sewing, shopping and every form of secretarial work, including *The Field Afar*.

Only in the mid-1940's did the sisters begin to curtail these services for the Society. The hiring of a new person as the printer, who also handled the mailing, gave Mother Mary Joseph an opportunity to withdraw the sisters from routine tasks at the magazine.

Over the next twenty years, the Maryknoll Sisters gradually ceased performing most of the household work for the Maryknoll Society, but continued the work with *The Field Afar* on many different levels.

Beginning in April 1939, *The Field Afar* was renamed:

Maryknoll – The Field Afar.

The complete turnover and change to the name
Maryknoll was on the 50th Anniversary of the Magazine in 1957.

A Reflective Moment
The purpose of *The Field Afar* was to vitalize
the missionary spirit in its readers.
Mother Mary Joseph said:
"May no one take us for anything but missioners!"
What is deepening our mission charism today?

Resources
The above Reflections were adapted from:
The Teresian Diaries;
Maryknoll in China by Jean-Paul Wiest;
Maryknoll's First Lady
by Jeanne Marie Lyons, MM;
To the Uttermost Parts of the Earth
by Camilla Kennedy, MM;
Hearts on Fire by Penny Lernoux;
and Archival Documents.

೮೦   ೮೦   ೮೦

IHM Sisters Gerard, Domitilla and Stanislaus pictured with some of the Teresians. Mollie (Mary Joseph) is on the right in the back row.

#9 ~ Thinking of the Future and Religious Life

Even in those hectic early years Mollie was thinking of the future, to a time when Maryknoll women, as well as men, would serve in foreign missions. Father Walsh's original idea had been to use the Teresians as auxiliaries to keep the seminary going, much as similar women's organizations helped European missionary societies. But since her days at Smith, Mollie had always nurtured the hope that young women would go overseas. The idea of starting a new community of religious women for foreign missions evolved naturally from the first goal. As Mollie admitted, she had been attracted to foreign missions since childhood but not to the sisterhood. Nevertheless, the atmosphere at Maryknoll, with the heavy emphasis on spirituality, encouraged the women's religious sensibilities.

Shortly after the women had arrived at Maryknoll in 1912, Father Walsh had given them a schedule that was nearly as exacting as a formal novitiate ~ the day started at 5:30 a.m., and continued with prayers, work and recreation till 9:30 at night when the exhausted women fell into bed. But there was always a certain flexibility ~ if *The Field Afar* had to be mailed that day, prayers had to wait.

Communities Contacted

In 1913 it was still not obvious just how the secretaries would go about becoming a religious congregation. Father Walsh realized at the very least they would need the authorization of a bishop as well as initial formation in religious life. For this, he favored the Franciscan Missionaries of Mary, whom he had seen at work in the mission field and whose spirit he had greatly admired. Father wrote a request to the sisters. After a description of the location of the Maryknoll Seminary, he said:

"In House number two, we have the office of our paper, The Field Afar, with seven women consecrated to the work of a literary propaganda." Though he did not mention Mary Joseph by name, he singled her out as the one in charge who *"just reached thirty....is finely educated, has a great heart, a child's faith and is much loved by the others."* He pointed to her lack of any religious training except as a laywoman.

After a long time of waiting due to a then unknown miscarriage of mail, Father Walsh received a negative reply, dated February 14, 1914, from the Mother General which read in part: *"As I never received the letter dated the month of August, of which you have sent me a copy, I thought that you had given up your scheme in as far as it concerned us, and I therefore sent to the Missions those Religious whom I had chosen for you."*

The Immaculate Heart of Mary Sisters

Father Walsh approached six other religious communities before receiving a favorable reply from the Sisters Servants of the Immaculate Heart of Mary in Scranton, PA. On May 25, 1914, Father James A Walsh wrote to Mother Germaine, the Mother General, asking for sisters to train the nine laywomen at Maryknoll. He began: *"We have here at present nine lay women, ranging in years from nineteen to over forty. They are giving their service gratis to the cause of Foreign Missions. Some are very well-educated, others much less so, but all are intelligent and, during the past two years at Maryknoll have given splendid evidence that they can cooperate unto good."*

Father mentioned that Cardinal Farley had visited the Teresians and granted the privilege of daily Mass, then the reservation of the Blessed Sacrament, and later Benediction. His Eminence had also suggested the uniform which they wear. Father Walsh ended by saying: *"I believe that three sisters will be enough, one to be Superior and Mistress of Novices, another to manage the household affairs (this would include also the Seminary kitchen), and a third to supervise laundry, etc. We are willing to pay twenty dollars a month, with board, for each sister and will make the accommodations as comfortable as our space and means permit. Please let me know at your earliest convenience the decision, and may you be directed for God's greater glory."* Mary Joseph followed up this letter by going to Scranton about June 15 to see Bishop Hoban and to talk over details with Mother Germaine.

Julia Ward and Trip to Europe

Meanwhile, among the Teresians' friends was a well-to-do fashion designer, Julia Ward, whose name frequently appeared on New York theater programs and whose clients included such popular stars as the actress Maude Adams. Julia greatly admired Mollie, and she helped the Teresians with generous gifts, including the famous lobsters, as well as such practical items as winter hats and screens for St. Teresa's Lodge.

Julia wanted Mollie to accompany her on a trip to Europe, and Father Walsh, who saw how hard Mollie worked, thought it would be a good change for her and would assuredly broaden her vision of the Catholic tradition. When the invitation was extended, Mollie found herself faced with a solid front of approval and a formal resolution insisting that she accept, signed by the Teresians and Father Walsh as "commander-in-chief," and approved by Cardinal Farley! Mollie, herself, felt it would be an awkward time to be away because the Immaculate Heart Sisters were soon to arrive at Maryknoll. Out of courtesy she brought the matter to the superior, Mother Germaine, who also saw it as an opportunity that would benefit the entire group. Mary Joseph's experiences, especially in Rome, would indeed mark the development of the congregation in very significant ways.

Lourdes and Rome

Mary Joseph and Julia Ward sailed for France on July 15, 1914, less than a month after the murder of the heir to the throne of Austria-Hungary, Archduke Ferdinand and his wife Sophie, by a Serbian Nationalist. Unaware that the assassinations would spark an international war, the women journeyed with other pilgrims to Lourdes, arriving on July 28, the very day war was declared. Mary Joseph was deeply moved by the daily stream of sick and disabled people at the Grotto, helped by nurses and aides with obviously tender care. In the evenings she and Julia Ward joined the thousands of other pilgrims in the procession from the Grotto through the esplanade, singing the Lourdes *Ave, Ave, Ave Maria*. A few days after their arrival, they heard the mayor read mobilization orders for the war with Germany.

The women eventually made their way to Italy. By the time they reached Rome, Pope Pius X was dying, which occurred on August 20, 1914, and they were present for his funeral and the election of a new pope, Benedict XV. They joined the large crowd waiting in Saint Peter's Square to see the puff of white smoke announcing the election of a new pope. They were stranded in Rome for an extra month because of the war, giving Mollie a sense of the grandeur and history of the Roman Catholic Church.

Visit to Hospital of Company of Mary

Going with Julia to see a sick friend at the Hospital of the Company of Mary, Mollie went into the chapel. Before the altar a white-veiled, blue-habited novice knelt praying. Presently another novice came forward, the two genuflected together, the first one left the chapel and the second took her place. Later on, one of the sisters informed Mollie, *"While some sisters are out working for the poor and the sick, someone is always praying for us. How beautiful,"* Mollie thought, *"If only we too could do something like that."*

Mollie pictured the chapel and the handful of women in the old farmhouse at home, thinking to herself: *"Not now, maybe later."* This desire would confirm Mollie's conviction that every Maryknoll Sister is called to be a contemplative in mission, as well as having perpetual adoration at the Motherhouse Chapel early in the Congregation's history, and a contemplative community within the Congregation to pray for the missions.

Arrival of the IHM Sisters

Three Immaculate Heart of Mary Sisters (IHM): Sister M. Stanislaus, Sister M. Gerard and Sister M. Domitilla arrived at Maryknoll to begin the Teresians' formalized religious training on September 15, 1914. Mary Joseph was still in Europe. Almost immediately the Teresians perceived a difference. A new ordering which they referred to as *convent training* commenced. Mary Louise captured the experience in her diary account with these words:

> *The Seminary opened its third year with a High Mass in honor of the Holy Spirit, but we did not attend, as Mother Germaine told us we were not to go to services except in our own chapel hereafter....We began to wash dishes in convent fashion, each one attending to her own. Our first attempts were very awkward but the system will certainly save us time when we learn. The Immaculate Heart of Mary Sisters began to hope for the end of The Field Afar magazine. They do not yet know what our monthly mailing means.*

Guided by the Immaculate Heart of Mary Sisters

Although the Teresians tried to live up to the rules of the IHM Sisters, the relationship was often strained. The more democratic Teresians found it difficult to accept a situation in which there was no discussion and the superior's command was absolute law, which was present at that time in most communities. Meals and recreation were governed by a strict hierarchy, from oldest to youngest. Penances, such as kissing the superior's feet, were often practiced, which was the custom in some communities.

With the passage of days, the Teresians yearned for Mary Joseph's homecoming from Europe. She had written from Rome about the death of Pope Pius X and the poor conditions in Europe because of the outbreak of World War I.

Mollie Joins the Novitiate

On her return to Maryknoll on October 2, 1914, Mollie found the three Immaculate Heart of Mary Sisters already at Maryknoll, and the Teresians making a month-old effort to acquire the sedate ways and virtues they considered proper to novices. During the first month they had all gone through a period of discouragement. After having been given two days to talk about her trip to Europe, Mary Joseph then became a novice in training with the other Teresians. She joined them in all the novitiate exercises, listened to the instructions that began each day, adopted all the practices suggested, carried out the penances, observed the unaccustomed old-world formalities between subject and superior. With Mary Joseph present, the new yoke seemed to lie more lightly on them all.

Mollie and The Field Afar

However awkward some of these practices may have seemed to Mollie as well, they did not inhibit her spontaneity. Even as a novice she repeatedly demonstrated her genius for maintaining a balance between the demands of religious observance and the urgent work at hand. It was not long before the Immaculate Heart Sisters *began to hope for the end of The Field Afar,* which it seemed to them, was unduly distracting the novices. Mary Joseph and all the Teresians realized that the Immaculate Heart Sisters could not have known beforehand that the mailing of *The Field Afar* was a task that consumed a substantial number of days every month. As Mary Joseph had done years before within the Rogers' family, here again she deftly drew on her talent to offset potential conflicts by helping the IHMs understand how vital this mailing was for the life and continuation of the Foreign Mission Society.

Consideration of Religious Orders

As the year 1915 came and went and the formal religious training with the Immaculate Heart of Mary Sisters moved into its second year, the Teresians began a consideration of religious orders. Their experience up to now taught them their need for a religious rule which offered a degree of flexibility. Very early in 1912, Father John McNicholas, OP, had suggested to Father Walsh the Dominican Rule for the women.

It would have been premature at that time, but it was now apropos for Mary Joseph, Sister Stanislaus, IHM, and Father Walsh to give this idea some serious thought. Mary Joseph wrote a request to Father McNicholas for a copy of the Dominican Third Order Rules. She also made a similar request to the Carmelites.

Devotion to St. Teresa to Be Kept

Mary Joseph and the Teresians were drawn to the Carmelites because of their growing knowledge and love of St. Teresa of Avila, their patroness. After Mary Joseph had talked individually with each Teresian about the subject of rules, she obtained an expression of opinion in writing. All approved of the Dominican Rule provided devotion to St. Teresa might be kept. Mary Joseph informed Father McNicholas, OP:

"We have practically decided to take up the Dominican idea and all are willing and happy to accept whatever seems best to Father Walsh who, as you know, is inclined your way." The decision to be Dominican resulted in Father McNicholas, O.P., being appointed by Cardinal John Farley *"to take up the organization of the Teresians as a community of Dominican Tertiaries,"* with the advice and direction of Father Walsh.

Training by Immaculate Heart of Mary Sisters Not Canonical

It was soon discovered by Father McNicholas that the religious training of the Teresians by the Immaculate Heart of Mary Sisters was *"not canonical."* He came to Maryknoll on March 7, 1916. He first explained to the Teresians that:

> *According to a recent decree, permission to start any religious congregation must come from Rome ~ a fact to which Cardinal Farley did not advert and which even the Apostolic Delegate did not appreciate.*

This meant that technically the eighteen months' novitiate did not count but would be invaluable as well as a help in whatever supplementary training might be necessary. Father McNicholas then went over the obligations of Dominican Tertiaries and enrolled the Teresians in the scapular ~ not as a body but as individuals. So, despite the setback in one direction, the Teresians had moved another step in the decision-making toward religious life. They had decided to belong to the Dominican Family.

Religious Names Taken

On May 3, 1916, each of the Teresians, with the approval of Father Walsh, took a religious name, although they could use the title "Sister" only at Maryknoll: Mary Louise Wholean chose "Mary Xavier," Sara Sullivan "Mary Teresa," Nora Shea, "Mary Theophane," Margaret Shea "Mary Gemma," and Anna Towle "Anna Maria."

IHM Sisters Leave

On June 30, 1916, a farewell supper was held for the IHM Sisters. The refectory was decorated with Chinese lanterns. Father Walsh was invited and expressed pleasure in being with the group. He thanked the IHM Sisters for their example of labor and humility and having a strong faith in God. The next morning the sisters made an early start for Scranton.

A new chapter had begun in the Life of the Teresians!

The Teresians had decided to belong to the Dominican Family, because their missionary vocation was most compatible with the Dominican ideal of contemplation in action, and the flexibility of their Rule.

A Reflective Moment

As the Teresians lived through many unknowns, how does their witness empower us today?

Resources

The above Reflections were adapted from:
Maryknoll's First Lady by Jeanne Marie Lyons, MM;
To the Uttermost Parts of the Earth
by Camilla Kennedy, MM;
Hearts on Fire by Penny Lernoux;
and *On the Threshold of the Future*
by Claudette LaVerdiere, MM; and
As One Lamp Lights Another
by Barbara Hendricks, MM.

℘   ℘   ℘

#10 ~ Some Events from 1915 to 1920

St. Teresa's Day in 1915
The Tin Lizzie above, politely called *'Elizabeth'* and chauffeured, tradition says, by Seminarian Frank Ford who later became Bishop of Kaying, China, was their means of going out on special occasions, such as this outing to Far Rockaway on St. Teresa's Day. The man walking around the front of the car was Father James A. Walsh.

The Teresians and Recreation

And of course, the Teresians were so exuberant ~ they loved parties, storytelling and jokes, and during free periods they had a good time talking and singing, even though recreation consisted of stringing beans or darning the seminarians' socks. The Maryknoll women were often entertained by a young Teresian nicknamed *"The Clown,"* who had an ample repertoire of song and dance and operatic burlesque. Irrepressible, she once presented Father James A. Walsh with a bouquet of vegetables after he had given a talk on martyrs!

On the night of a sister's feast day, the Teresians celebrated with a costume ball with kimonos trimmed with ribbons and tinsel. Mollie, who was supposed to be the austere founder of a strict religious order, showed up with giant emerald earrings made from Christmas tree candle holders.

Also in the early days, occasionally the local Undertaker from Dorsey Funeral Home in Ossining took the Teresians for a drive in his hearse!

Tradition of Ice Cream Sodas

On October 15, 1915, Mary Joseph started a Maryknoll tradition by celebrating St. Teresa's Feast Day with ice cream sodas. She secretly set up a soda fountain and booths in the garden, but Margaret Shea, unaccustomed to handling such a large bottle of soda, managed to spray it all over the kitchen before the party started, and another had to be purchased. The soda fountain offered such tempting concoctions as *Ningpo Sundae* and *Chop Suey,* with Mary Joseph and Margaret serving as soda jerks. In what also became a Maryknoll custom, the party was followed by three-legged sack races and dancing. There were birthday parties, plays, picnics and outings to Rye Beach, where the women went swimming in the tank suits of the time!

1916-1920 Years of Struggle for Official Recognition from Rome

From 1913 to 1916, eleven more women had joined the Teresians. They came to a decision in 1916 to be women religious as Dominicans, and they struggled from 1916 to 1920 to obtain official recognition from Rome. Correspondence among Cardinal John Farley, Father James Anthony Walsh, Father John McNicholas, OP, and Mollie directed the process of application. Great care was exercised so that it would not be when we thought our work finished, it might be discovered we had built on an invalid foundation. The struggle of these years is focused in the historical perspective of three petitions which were sent to Rome by the Teresians for approval.

The First Petition

In compliance with the official Roman procedure, Monsignor Ferrante of the Sacred Congregation of Religious in Rome prepared in Italian the first petition. It was a very simple request to open a novitiate at St. Teresa's under the title of Dominican Tertiaries of the Foreign Missions. It was first sent to Rome on June 30, 1916. It was returned as Father Walsh noted: "*Because it was addressed to the Congregation of Propaganda rather than to that of Regulars.*"

Actually, Father McNicholas, OP, had advised sending the request to the Congregation of Regulars, but the diocesan canonist judged otherwise. The petition was re-addressed and re-sent to Rome on August 17, 1916. By January 16, 1917, a reply to this first petition was received by Cardinal Farley at the New York Chancery. It granted the Teresians the right to be organized as a pious society "*bound by no religious vows.*" It was unexpected and a very great disappointment to the Teresians. In fact, it "*amounted to a refusal,*" in their minds.

Mollie's Response

Mollie expressed her own reaction in a note to Father Walsh: *"The shock of the announcement, which was almost panic, is over and I can see things more clearly. I believe the Teresians as a body will willingly accept the decision. To do otherwise would be to wound the Head of which we are members. It will be a good test of our Catholicity, our vocation and our love."*

It was necessary to make adjustments. Mollie wrote in January 1917 about the *'new conditions'* to Sister Ruth, O.P., in Sinsinawa, whose plan was all set to come to Maryknoll to form the Teresians along Dominican lines. Mollie's letter noted that despite the negative reply from Rome, they all desired her to come.

Spiritual Formation

These early women had come to Maryknoll with the determination and a heart's desire to be missioners. Those who came obviously had courage. Now, added to that innate strength, was a spiritual formation based on two very strong women of the Church — first St. Teresa of Avila and now with the Sinsinawa Dominicans, St. Catherine of Siena. Catherine's example and teaching of a life of contemplation and action were a strong foundation for each and all of the *Pious Women*.

Years later, Mother Mary Joseph would explain it this way:

Our life was a busy, distracted one ~ each day far too short to see its tasks completed. We soon learned that a missioner must be a contemplative in action; that our hearts must be on fire with love of God and souls. Meditation, faithfulness to times of prayer and trying to be constantly mindful of God's presence in our souls were the foundation of this missionary life we had chosen to follow, a life so busy that we often wondered - as we do even today - how we could live at once a life of prayer and a life of extreme activity. St. Teresa obtained that gift for us, I truly believe, and so, laid the foundation for our Dominican life that combines perfectly the ways of prayer and activity.

Mary Louise Wholean

At the end of her letter to Sister Ruth, O.P., Mollie wrote this poignant line: *"One of the Teresians (Mary Louise Wholean), the first to join, is near death and I doubt if she can live many days."* Just when the Teresians were gaining momentum to realize their dream, Mary Louise Wholean became bedridden. Nothing could be done for her cancer.

Throughout the years, illness had become a familiar companion to Mary Louise, who agonized through a long, painful illness from incurable stomach cancer. Mollie acted as infirmarian, especially when the duties were heavy. All throughout the fall and winter of 1916, Mary Louise struggled bravely with her illness. She wrote her last entry in the *Teresian Diary* on December 21, 1916. As the new year began, she was bedridden and growing emaciated almost beyond recognition. She had not yielded up her dream to continue the work to which she was so devoted. All at Maryknoll knew she was dying except Mary Louise herself. Her mother came to be with her during those last weeks.

Mollie took on the duties of night nurse and watched and prayed over the unequal battle, bringing such serenity and insight into the sickroom that the dying woman hung on to her presence as if she might drown without it. By day Mollie carried on as much of her usual work as she was able and snatched what rest she could.

When, on February 19, 1917, death finally came to Mary Louise at age thirty-five, it found her ready, her resistance laid aside, her own dream of serving God abandoned fully and finally in favor of God's plan for her. It was a great grace. From it, Mollie drew much consolation even while she felt keenly this first death among her companions. For both Mary Joseph and Father Walsh, as well as all the Teresians, Mary Louise's death in February was a great loss and a heartrending event.

Excerpt from Father Walsh's Eulogy

Father James Anthony Walsh's eulogy spoke eloquently of the incalculable loss Mary Louise's death meant for all of Maryknoll. She loved Maryknoll, he said, as a mother loves her child, or, as she remarked a few days before her death, "*every foot of it.*" As her mother sat at her daughter's bedside reading the February issue of *The Field Afar,* the sufferer's eyes turned toward the paper and asked that it be read to her. The mother answered that she was looking for something interesting, and she whose death we were hourly expecting, said with emphasis, "*Why it is all interesting!*" ~ a remark characteristic of the deep affection which she had for every activity at Maryknoll.

The Holy Spirit had breathed upon her soul. God had chosen her. She suffered bravely and bore it to the end. Her heart was a heart of gold, affectionate and loyal. Our first representative has gone from Maryknoll to be our intercessor – she who has offered her life for this work.

Mollie's Illnesses

Worn out by Mary Louise's long illness, Mollie remained tired all that late winter and spring. Soon illness came to be her companion. At home it had been almost unknown for her to be sick. Now she embarked upon the first of a long series of illnesses that would pace themselves over the rest of her life like the way of the cross. They would not prevent her working, nor take away her joy in giving herself to the task at hand. When she had to submit to hospitalization and surgery, she would do so with such humor and relaxation that many, even the sisters who nursed her, had no realization of her pain and weakness. The effortless way in which she detached her mind from herself and fastened it on the concerns and needs of others, particularly evident toward the end of her life, was the fruit of long habit, as well as Mollie's walking in the way of love throughout her life.

During the spring and summer of 1917, she made a slow and difficult recovery from an abdominal operation, at one time burning with fever and weighed down with pain, at another improving only to relapse again. After several months, the body finally responded, and the infection was sealed off and healed, and she was able to take up her full round of activity.

Mary Augustine Dwyer

Since the fall of 1913, Mary Augustine, one of the three secretaries who had arrived on January 6, 1912, had been acting as bookkeeper, secretary and housekeeper at the Venard Apostolic School in Scranton, the nucleus of a Junior Seminary begun at that time by Father James A. Walsh. Even the virtual independence of this position, and the opportunities it gave her considerable abilities, left her dissatisfied. On June 14, 1914, Mollie left for Scranton where she was to help Mary Augustine close up the house for the summer, spend a few days with the Sisters of the Immaculate Heart of Mary, call on Bishop Hoban, and attend to various matters for which she asked the Teresians to remember in prayer.

Mollie was grieved to find how much Mary Augustine's discontent had overflowed into criticism of Father Walsh's way of developing the group of women auxiliaries. The difficulties which she created for Father Walsh pained Mollie more than any of the suffering which Mary Augustine caused her personally. She had two key complaints. First of all, she felt the Teresians lacked definiteness. They had no real rule, no status, no stable organization. Mollie replied: *"You know as much of the future as I do. God has provided for us thus far. Why should God fail us now?"*

Mary Augustine's second complaint concerned the composition of the group itself. Some of the Teresians were trained and some were untrained. She felt that the community of women needed to be in two separate groups: one with skilled office workers and one with domestic workers. Mollie, holding deep pain in her heart at hearing this kind of complaint, replied gently but firmly. *"We can never have any such division among us!"*

Mollie, and later as Mother Mary Joseph, always envisioned the Maryknoll Sisters Community as one family, with a great variety of gifts and diversity of cultures and personalities. Having a heart to love and a will to serve were the main requisites of our Maryknoll mission vocation.

In April of 1916, Mary Augustine Dwyer chose to return to Boston and she successfully re-established her former business. Mollie always appreciated Mary Augustine's hard work and the great contribution she made in the early days. Also, Father James A. Walsh visited her whenever he was in Boston.

A Reflective Moment
As we are exposed to difficulties
within and beyond our Community,
do we experience these trials as being
integral to deepening and strengthening
our call to universal communion?

Resources
The above Reflections were adapted from:
Maryknoll's First Lady by Jeanne Marie Lyons, MM;
To the Uttermost Parts of the Earth
by Camilla Kennedy, MM;
Hearts on Fire by Penny Lernoux;
As One Lamp Lights Another by Barbara Hendricks, MM;
The Spirituality of Mollie Rogers by Elizabeth Carr, Ph.D.;
Teresian Diary and *Archival Material*.

೮೦   ೮೦   ೮೦

#11 ~ Preparing for Canonical Status

Sister Ruth Devlin, OP, Sister Fidelia Delaney, OP,
Mother Mary Joseph, MM and Sister Magdalen Doelger, MM.

Sister Ruth Devlin, O.P., Arrives from Sinsinawa, Wisconsin

Before the Teresians received Rome's negative reply to their first petition to open a canonical novitiate, the Dominican Sisters of Sinsinawa had already agreed to send Sister Ruth Devlin to assist in their spiritual formation. Mary Joseph wrote to assure her that despite the disappointing refusal by Rome, the Teresians' invitation held firm. Sister Ruth responded by coming to Maryknoll from April to August, 1917, to teach Dominican prayers, customs and the fundamentals of Dominican spirituality. Mollie and Sister Ruth discussed and worked over the proposed constitutions together. Even though Sister Ruth was with the Teresians only from April to August, she was instrumental in helping them lay a solid foundation for the future congregation. She and Mollie had much in common, and during their brief association formed a lasting friendship.

Preparing for the Second Petition

In 1917 Father Walsh traveled to China in search of a mission for the first group of Maryknoll priests. Before his departure, he helped formulate a second petition for the recognition of the Teresians as a religious community, signed by Cardinal Farley. This was mailed to Rome with a recommendation by Father Theissling, Master General of the Dominican Order.

During her stay with the Teresians, Sister Ruth also helped Mollie work toward the preparation of the Teresians' second petition to Rome to be women religious. After Sister Mary Ruth's departure in August 1917, Mollie was once again in the position of the Director of the Teresians.

Mollie wrote to Father McNicholas, O.P., about what had been accomplished during Sister Ruth's time with them:

She (Sr. Ruth), Father Walsh and I translated and adapted the St. Catherine Rule you so kindly sent. The Constitutions are now ready in English and French, and Father Walsh has written to His Eminence requesting him to examine them personally, or by deputy, and if they are approved, to prepare a second petition which is, if possible, to be sent directly to you.

The work is growing, our numbers are increasing ~ we shall be twenty-five by September 1st (1917) ~ our Apostolic School (Venard) needs such help as we can give, and yet we cannot do much until permission comes to open our canonical novitiate and some have completed the term. You may imagine how hard we are praying.

The Second Petition

The second petition was formally prepared by Father McNicholas, O.P., signed by Cardinal Farley, recommended by Father Theissling, the Dominican Master General, and dated October 22, 1917. Then the Teresians' period of waiting began for the second time. After months passed, on July 18, 1918, Monsignor Ferrante of the Sacred Congregation of Religious communicated the second refusal on the grounds that the scope of the work and means of support were not clearly defined. The Roman statement, dated February 7, 1918, stated that careful consideration upheld the same decision as that of November 25, 1916. Rome had not moved.

The Year 1918

The year 1918 was packed full of activities for the women at Maryknoll. They expanded their program of preserving and canning the produce raised on the farm. *The Field Afar* continued to increase in readership, demanding more and more hours of work. A steady stream of young women had arrived at St. Teresa's hoping to become involved in foreign missions.

On July 16, 1918, the thirteen Teresians who had been there the longest made private vows to Father Charles J. Callan, OP, a scripture scholar at the Seminary. The same day four Teresians departed for Scranton, where they opened their first mission at Clark's Green. By the end of the year there would be twenty-five Teresians working and praying together to become foreign missioners. To add to the joy of that year, World War I ended in November and Mary Joseph's three brothers, who were in the Armed Forces, returned home safely.

The Death of Father Thomas F. Price

On September 7, 1918, the first group of Maryknoll Fathers left for Yeungkong. Father Thomas Price, co-founder, led the group of young priests: Fathers James E. Walsh, Francis X. Ford and Bernard F. Meyer. Father Price was fifty-eight years old. Word reached Maryknoll that Father Price had died in Hong Kong on September 12, 1919, within a year of his arrival in China. Stricken with acute appendicitis, Father Price was buried in Hong Kong. His body would be taken for burial next to Father James A. Walsh after the latter's death in 1936. Expressions of sympathy, accompanied by prayers, flowed into Maryknoll from all over the United States.

Prelude to the Third Petition

The refusal of Rome for the second time to the petition for the Teresians to organize as religious caused great concern particularly to Father Walsh, Mary Joseph and the Teresians themselves. Father Walsh wrote letters to people who might be able to influence the process.

With a sense of urgency, he wrote to Monsignor Laurenti at the Society of the Propagation of the Faith in Rome:

The good women of whom I speak, now twenty-five in number, are not impatient, but in their present condition they cannot encourage additions to their ranks, although vocations are numerous. They are hoping from day to day to begin a Canonical Novitiate, at the end of which they can send members to other parts of the country.

A few months later Father Walsh wrote a request to Father McNicholas, O.P., now the Bishop of Duluth, Minnesota, to draft a new petition, the third one. He stated, *"The Foreign Mission Sisters of St. Dominic, claim my first thought now,"* and listed the sequence of official correspondence with Rome from the fact of the first petition in March, 1916, to his own letter to Monsignor Laurenti in May of 1918. He located the work of the Teresians in its relation to the Catholic Foreign Mission Society:

"I can say with all truth that their zealous and intelligent labor is practically indispensable in our work...." His letter closed with a fact of great import: *"Our missioners have already found an opening for women-workers at Yeungkong."* The mission field awaited the Teresians, but they were held fast by Rome and unable to move.

Preparation of Third Petition

After taking her vows on July 16, Mollie worked on the preparation of the third petition. She informed Bishop McNicholas, O.P., in regard to the tentative draft of the Constitutions which she was sending him. She also emphasized the movement in following the constitutions *"as well as we can. We separated the novices from the senior sisters and appointed a novice mistress....we are still saying the Office in English."* The work of the third petition was in process for a full year. It was completed by June 7, 1919, and hand carried to Rome by the Apostolic Delegate, Archbishop Bonzano.

Sister Fidelia Delaney, O.P.

Although the formal novitiate year could not yet begin since Rome had not yet spoken, Mother Mary Samuel of the Sinsinawa Dominicans was willing to send Sister Fidelia Delaney, nearly sixty years old, who arrived on July 15, 1919, to begin the necessary formation program in anticipation of a favorable response from Rome. Mary Joseph saw Sister Fidelia as a sister of ripe experience having been a religious for forty-three years and who held responsible offices in the Congregation.

Sister Fidelia was balanced in judgment, and distinguished easily and precisely between what belonged to the essence of religious life and what pertained to individual community custom. She brought with her the best of the Dominican tradition and quickly captured the spirit and purpose of Maryknoll. She fit in so well that Father Walsh called her *Maryknoll's Grandmother* and her influence was profound. She had the remarkable gift of joining her novices in their voyage of discovery as they moved toward mission. Mary Joseph wrote:

> *Sister Fidelia brought to her work a brilliant mind, lofty ideals, the charm of a warm, loving heart, a delightful fund of humor, an immense generosity, deep humility, wells of common sense, and a most attractive, vitalizing spirituality. With consummate skill, she took things as she found them, and transformed them. She taught us to intensify our time of prayer, to properly motivate our work, to recreate with a free joyous spirit. She made sure we knew and understood our catechism.*

The Teresians found that they had acquired a great treasure in Sister Fidelia. Again, Mary Joseph was a novice. Thirty-six years old now and used to overseeing the Teresians with Father Walsh's direction, she accepted her role gratefully and completely, as novice and directress. The Teresians gratefully remembered the lovely relationship between Mary Joseph and Sister Fidelia.

Letter of Father Walsh to Cardinal Van Rossum in Rome
Early in 1920, Father Walsh again wrote to Cardinal Van Rossum
in Rome for approval for the Teresians:

....In a former letter, Your Eminence showed interest in the Sodality of women to whom we owe much in the progress of our own institute. I recall to Your Eminence that these women, who now number 42, and have been living under the spiritual direction of experienced Dominican nuns, following the rule of Dominican Tertiaries, have been recognized by Rome as a 'Piam Societatem Mulierum' without vows.

They desire vows and a petition to this effect, carefully prepared by Bishop McNicholas, OP, former secretary to Father Theissling, the Dominican General, and signed by the Archbishop of New York, was carried to Rome last June by Archbishop Bonzano, our beloved Apostolic Delegate, who personally presented it to the Congregation of Religious. These faithful helpers, who are known as the Foreign Mission Sisters of St. Dominic, now hope for an early reply. In the meantime, however, several fields are opening to them in work for the Chinese and Japanese of this country. Our own missioners, under advice of Bishop DeGuebriant, also look forward to their going to China within the next two years. It would be most desirable if their final status could be settled before they take up several branches of work, but I do not know what we can do to further their cause. If the fuller approval does not come soon, may we encourage them to prepare for work in China, without waiting for the more formal novitiate with canonical vows?

Mary Joseph Receives the Good News
On February 14, 1920, Mary Joseph returned from a short stay at Trinity College, Washington, D.C., where she had gone to give a mission talk. She found St. Teresa's Lodge bubbling over with high spirits with the good news from Rome! Mary Francis Davis had answered the telephone and received the message on February 12. She explained to Mary Joseph that Monsignor Dunn phoned saying he could not get the Seminary, and he needed to speak with Father Walsh about a very important message Archbishop Hayes had received from Rome. He asked her to bring this good news to him and not to tell anyone else first. Mary Francis said to Mary Joseph: *"How could I go rushing over to the Seminary without saying a word to anyone? So I told Sister Fidelia and then Mary Teresa, and then we did get word to the Seminary. We got everyone together here and told them. They put me on top of the table and had me announce the whole thing."* Then Mary Teresa said: *"Did you tell Mary Joseph that you did a dance right on top of the table?"* Mary Francis replied: *"I was carried away. Isn't it wonderful!"*

Recognition by Rome

It was wonderful and uplifting for everyone! In a letter dated January 10, 1920, the Sacred Congregation gave Archbishop Hayes the full faculties to establish the Teresians into a diocesan religious institute, which he did in a document dated February 14, 1920, the official Canonical Foundation Day of the Foreign Mission Sisters of St. Dominic. On February 17, 1920, Monsignor Dunn handed the official document from Rome to Father Walsh, who in turn passed it on to Mary Joseph, who loved every syllable of its staid legal language. Thus, another outstanding event in the life of Mary Joseph had come to pass. She was thirty-eight when the Community was recognized by Rome, and she was profoundly grateful for God's great gift of Maryknoll!

Hopes and Dreams

1920 was filled with new hopes and dreams for the Teresians. Their uniforms were replaced by grey habits, scapulars, white veils and silver medals of the Blessed Virgin Mary. In *The Field Afar,* Father Walsh began to refer to them as *the Maryknoll Sisters* ~ a short form of the *Foreign Mission Sisters of St. Dominic.*

Sister Mary Francis Davis

On December 28, 1914, Elsie Frances St. Claire Davis (Sr. M. Francis), proficient in secretarial work, was the 14th member to join the Teresians, entering from Brooklyn, NY. She was of mixed blood and the first African-American. She was born in Jersey City, NJ, on July 23, 1889, and was in the first group professed in 1921, and in the second group assigned to China in 1922. Sister was chosen as one of the delegates from China to attend the First Congregational Chapter in 1925. However, she and Sisters Paul McKenna and Magdalen Doelger were unable to get transport, but each had a Chapter delegate as a proxy to vote for them. After 18 years in China and 4 years in Manila, she returned to the States, doing secretarial work at the Sisters' Center and at *The Field Afar* office from 1944 to 1957. Like her companions of those early days, she gave herself generously and joyfully to the work of the community, and watched it grow with an ever-deepening love in her heart. Sister Mary Francis died peacefully at Bethany on October 12, 1966.

A Reflective Moment

Through the Teresians' patience and perseverance, the Maryknoll Sisters
became a reality. At this moment in our history,
what is being drawn forth from us, as recipients of this great gift?

The above Reflections were adapted from:

Maryknoll's First Lady by Jeanne Marie Lyons, MM;
To the Uttermost Parts of the Earth by Camilla Kennedy, MM;
On the Threshold of the Future by Claudette LaVerdiere, MM;
As One Lamp Lights Another by Barbara Hendricks, MM;
Hearts on Fire by Penny Lernoux; Archives-Obituary of Sister Mary Francis Davis;
Maryknoll in China by Jean-Paul Wiest.

ℵℂ   ℵℂ   ℵℂ

#12 ~ Some Events from 1920 to 1922

First Departure Ceremony to China ~ September 12, 1921
Bottom Row: Sisters M. Lawrence Foley, M. Paul Mc Kenna, Superior, M. Rose Leifels.
Standing: M. Imelda Sheridan, M. Barbara Froehlich, M. Monica Moffat.

Women Religious Missioners

The twenties began with the joyous news of the Teresians being approved by Rome as a diocesan religious institute on February 14, 1920, the official Canonical Foundation Day of the Foreign Mission Sisters of St. Dominic, who were now in fact the Maryknoll Sisters. It had taken the Teresians eight years to obtain recognition by Rome. During that time, with Mary Joseph as their Directress, they had evolved a simple lifestyle adapted completely to the many indispensable works connected to the growing foreign mission seminary, not least of which was the publication of *The Field Afar*. Their formal religious training was limited to one year and a half, and their Dominican formation to a short six months. Now, Sister Fidelia, O.P., a religious of forty-three years took up the work of training the community along Dominican lines, to be Maryknoll Dominicans.

The March and April 1920 issues of *The Field Afar* boasted the fact with feature articles. For the first time ever, the term *Maryknoll Sisters* was used to designate these women who were *formerly known to our readers as The Teresians*. For the first time ever, women, through an American-founded Community, will consecrate their lives to foreign missions, a milestone in the religious history of American Catholicism.

Some Local Assignments

Sister Mary Joseph called personally on Archbishop Hayes to obtain permission to send, in response to invitations received from Bishop Cantwell of Los Angeles and Bishop O'Dea of Seattle, the required number of sisters to conduct in their dioceses mission work for the Japanese. The permission was graciously given.

The Archbishop also heartily approved of the sisters starting their hospital training at the Ossining Hospital. The following local assignments were made:

April 3, 1920 ~ Three sisters were sent to Ossining Hospital to start nurses' training: sisters M. Michael Conlin, M. Gerard Gallagher and M. Teresita O'Donnell.

April, 8, 1920 ~ Sister M. Magdalen Doelger was appointed Superior in Los Angeles, CA, accompanied by Sister Aloysius McDonald, and Sisters Gemma Shea and Gerard Gallagher went to Seattle, WA, a few weeks later.

May 30, 1920 ~ Formal opening of the Maryknoll Kindergarten for Japanese in Seattle with classes starting on June first.

October 1, 1920 ~ Sisters M. Lawrence Foley, Marie de Lourdes Bourguignon and M. Veronica Hartman were selected to take a short course in nursing at the Ossining Hospital.

February 11, 1921 ~ St. Teresa's Lodge (Convent) was designated as a Canonical Novitiate.

The First Profession of Vows

Sister Mary Joseph initiated the formal steps to meet the canonical requirements regarding the First Profession of Vows. She wrote to Archbishop Hayes who authored all necessary dispensations in a formal document dated February 3, 1921, and appointed her 'the first Prioress.' She would now be called Mother Mary Joseph and was placed in charge of the new institute for the first three years.

With the completion of one year of religious formation on February 15, 1921, Mother Mary Joseph, with twenty other sisters, professed their first vows at a ceremony held in St. Teresa's small chapel and Father James Anthony Walsh received their vows.

> *Twenty-one sisters made their vows that day, and for many in the group it was the crowning of almost a decade of patient waiting and unselfish devotion.*

It was a singular event of a marked historical significance. Rev. Thomas M. Schwertner, OP, gave the sisters' retreat before their profession.

The First Profession Group

Sr. Mary Joseph (Mary Josephine Rogers)
Sr. M. Teresa (Sara Teresa Sullivan)
Sr. M. Theophane (Nora Frances Shea)
Sr. Anna Maria (Anna Agnes Towle)
Sr. M. Catherine (Katherine Gertrude Fallon)
Sr. M. Ambrose (Mary Laetitia Crawford)
Sr. M. Francis (Elsie Frances Davis)
Sr. M. Agatha (Ellen Frances Davin)
Sr. M. Anthony (Nora Conway)
Sr. M. Rose (Anna Rose Leifels)
Sr. M. Patrick (Elinor Maher)
Sr. M. Elizabeth (Anna Regina Thompson)
Sr. M. Dolores (Mary Ann Cruise)
Sr. Margaret Mary (Katherine A. Slattery)
Sr. M. Paul (Grace Anselm McKenna)
Sr. M. Michael (Mary Ann Conlin)
Sr .M. Thomas (Brigid Mary Bresnahan)
Sr. M. John (Mary Ellen Troy Cahill)
Sr. M. Rita (Elizabeth Bodkin)
Sr. M. James (Louise Regis Rogers)
Sr. M. Philomena (Catherine Flanagan)

~ ~ ~

Mother Mary Joseph Visits Los Angeles and Seattle

In late December of 1920, Mother Mary Joseph wrote to Archbishop Hayes asking him to grant a dispensation for the ten sisters who had been willing to postpone their year of novitiate for the sake of the work at Scranton, Los Angeles and Seattle, so that they could be professed without having completed the novitiate. On Christmas Eve, the Archbishop granted the request.

In March 1921, Mother traveled by train to the Pacific coast to visit her two sisters in Los Angeles and two sisters in Seattle, to be with them as they took their vows and to acquaint herself with their work. The sisters in Los Angeles had been directed by Bishop Cantwell to take over the Home for Japanese Children which was formerly in charge of the *Sisters of the Visitation,* a Japanese religious community but without any canonical status.

On March 19, 1921, First Profession of our two sisters in Los Angeles took place: Sister M. Magdalen Doelger and Sister M. Aloysius McDonald. On April 13, 1921, First Profession of our two sisters in Seattle: Sister M. Gemma Shea and Sister M. Gerald Gallagher.

Mother Mary Joseph left the Pacific coast missions among the Japanese with great interest and high hopes of expanding the work. In Los Angeles Maryknoll Sisters would soon be responsible for staffing a home for Japanese children and a grade school, and in Seattle, a kindergarten in its early stages as well as a grade school. In both places there were needs for all kinds of social and pastoral services.

Sister Marianna Akashi

In early June 1921, when Mother returned from the West Coast to Maryknoll, Sister Marianna Akashi accompanied her, the first Japanese sister, born of Catholic parents, who had been a Novice in the Japanese Community, *Sisters of the Visitation*. Permission was granted by the Chancery to receive her privately into the Maryknoll Novitiate. On June 28, 1921, the eve of the Maryknoll Society's Tenth Anniversary of Foundation, Sister Marianna Akashi received the habit of a Maryknoll Sister in St. Teresa's Chapel.

Assignments ~ June 28, 1921

With the steady increase in numbers, Mother Mary Joseph and Father Walsh felt certain that it was time to send more sisters to the Pacific coast missions and to assign the first group to China. Before Benediction on the Eve of the Anniversary, after our Sister Marianna Akashi was received into the Congregation, Father James A. Walsh gave a brief reflection regarding assignments. He had a small piece of paper in his hand that Mother Mary Joseph had given him, and then he began to read the June 28, 1921, Assignments:

To the Venard: Sisters M. Thomas Bresnahan, M. Veronica Hartman, M. Stephen O'Donnell.

To Los Angeles: Sisters Elizabeth Thompson, M. Michael Conlin, M. Rita Bodkin, M. Philomena Flanagan, M. Gerard Gallagher, M. Teresita O'Donnell, M. Clare Miltenberger, and Postulant Ellen McMahon.

To Seattle: Sisters M. Anthony Conway, M. Aloysius McDonald and M. John Cahill.

For Nursing Training in Providence Hospital (Seattle): Sisters Marie de Lourdes Bourguignon, M. Ursula Kenkel and M. Mercedes Cusack.

First Pioneers to China: All were eagerly awaiting the names of the first Sisters to be assigned to China. No one seemed to move or breathe as the names were announced: Sisters M. Paul McKenna, Superior, M. Lawrence Foley, M. Barbara Froehlich, M. Rose Leifels, M. Monica Moffat and M. Imelda Sheridan.

The historical ceremony took place on September 12, 1921, with Archbishop Hayes, Monsignor John Dunn and Bishop Cassidy of Fall River, MA, who was the speaker. The ceremony was planned as a small private affair. However, old friends like Julia Ward and some of the sisters' relatives and friends crowded into the small fieldstone St. Martha's Chapel. Seating for the community stretched outdoors over the grass outside. Father James A. Walsh called forth the six sisters assigned to China. As each one approached the altar and once again pronounced her vows, she received from Father Walsh a crucifix which symbolized the call to mission in a life of love and sacrifice.

Mother Mary Joseph did everything she could to show her love, care and support for the newly-assigned to China. She planned little celebrations and provided gifts which would be of use in their missions. She went with them to New York City to secure their passports and tickets. It was a time of joy and fulfillment for Mother, yet it was also a time of impending separation and sorrow. This was something she would experience throughout her life when saying goodbye to her daughters leaving their home at Maryknoll for missions throughout the world.

The six Maryknoll Sisters, accompanied by Father Walsh and a priest friend from Boston, sailed on the S.S. Monteagle from Vancouver on September 24 and arrived in Kowloon, Hong Kong, on November 3, 1921. As far as the missioners knew, they perhaps would never see their homeland again. Before the year's end, the total number of Maryknoll Missioners in South China would reach twenty-four.

Kowloon and Yeungkong, South China

In August 1921 a second group of novices made their vows, bringing the total of professed sisters to thirty-eight. When more sisters were assigned to China in 1922, a group of sisters went to Yeungkong, arriving on November 20, 1922. Father Francis Xavier Ford put them in charge of what had traditionally been the responsibility of sisters all over China: a school, an orphanage, a house for a few old folks and blind girls, and some dispensary work. However, something happened which he had not anticipated. The sisters' arrival aroused much more interest among the local population than the presence of the male missioners.

In 1923, on the occasion of Mother Mary Joseph's first visit to China, Father Ford described the special attraction the women and children had for the sisters, and alluded for the first time to the important role religious women could fill in apostolic work with the women in the villages. When Father Ford shared his views with Mother, she too envisioned her sisters' pioneering a new approach of going out to the people. Her approval opened the way for the Maryknoll Sisters' direct apostolate in China, which blossomed in the 1930's.

The First Spiritual Conferences

On the Feast of All Saints in 1921, Mother Mary Joseph expressed her thoughts in what was the first of many letter-conferences sent to her sisters at the Venard, Los Angeles, Seattle and the six arriving in Hong Kong, and shared with all at Maryknoll, NY. She desired unity. Mother wrote:

> *As I told you recently, I hope to send you each month a few words of counsel on the same matters we shall consider on retreat day here so that we may all be united in our efforts to attain the love God requires of us.*

Mother fostered a loving spirit of unity in her ever constant and consistent exhortation to live day by day in the presence of God. She concluded: "*And if we do all for love of God, direct our intentions well, and consciously live in God's presence, we shall find that our day's acts show forth the other characteristics desired ~ zeal, devotedness, love for the sublime work to which we have been called ~ and we shall find nothing too hard, no sacrifice too great in the performance of our daily duties.*"

Each community had already received a copy of the *Exercises of St. Gertrude the Great*, the writings of the medieval Benedictine scholar and mystic. The texts Mother suggested for reflection from Exercises Six and Seven are filled with feelings of intimacy, longing and desire to serve God, "*with life-sustaining love.*" The following is an excerpt from Exercise Six:

> *O Unifying Love, God of my heart, love, praise, and jubilation of my spirit, my cherished One, let my spirit cling to You in one spirit, one breath, one will, one charity, until it becomes one spirit with You for eternity.*

In these letter-conferences, Mother hoped to continue the bond of a family spirit among her sisters no matter how far the Maryknoll Center in New York might be from wherever we are in mission.

Community Growth
By January 1, 1922:
The Community had 115 members:
38 Professed, 44 Novices and 33 Postulants.

By January 1, 1923:
The Community had 146 members:
58 Professed, 72 Novices and 16 Postulants.

First Three Sisters to Die
On February 19, 1917, Sister M. Xavier (Mary Louise Wholean) died of cancer at the age of 35. **On May 9, 1923,** Sister M. Emmanuel Donohue, a novice, died at the age of 23. Both professed their vows before they died, and were buried in St. Augustine Cemetery in Ossining, NY. **On August 21, 1923,** Sister Gertrude Moore, a nurse, while caring for typhoid patients in Yeungkong, died at the age of 28, and was buried in Yeungkong, China.

From The Field Afar – January 1919
General George Washington
Father James A. Walsh writes: *"We have been told that no less a personage than General George Washington, who became the first President of this truly great Republic, spent the night at what is now St. Teresa's Convent!"*

A Reflective Moment
Mother Mary Joseph carried in her heart
incredible concerns for housing and feeding
the growing community, and at the same time,
her spirituality deepened through her trust in God's Providence
and her selflessness in creating a family spirit.

Resources
The above Reflections were adapted from:
Maryknoll's First Lady by Jeanne Marie Lyons, MM;
To the Uttermost Parts of the Earth by Camilla Kennedy, MM;
Maryknoll in China by Jean-Paul Wiest;
#5 Spiritual Heritage of Mother Mary Joseph
by Barbara Hendricks, MM;
As One Lamp Lights Another by Barbara Hendricks
The Field Afar – 1919.

ෆ ෆ ෆ

#13 ~ Some Events from 1922 to 1924

Mother Mary Joseph with the Second Departure Group in 1922 to China: Sisters M. Dolores Cruise, M. Magdalen Doelger, M. Cecilia Cruickshank, M. Thomas Bresnahan, M. Gertrude Moore, Mother Mary Joseph and Sister M. Francis Davis.

Second Group of Sisters Leave for China

On September 12, 1922, the second group of sisters left for China. Led by Sister M. Magdalen Doelger, the group included: Sisters M. Dolores Cruise, M. Cecilia Cruickshank, M. Thomas Bresnahan, M. Francis Davis and M. Gertrude Moore, who was a registered nurse. They arrived in Hong Kong in October 1922, bringing six more sisters from Maryknoll where sixteen sisters had recently made their vows, so that the number of professed sisters in the Community now totaled fifty-five.

For a little while the Hong Kong house was bursting. However, some of the sisters were destined for a brand-new mission, Yeungkong, where Father Frank Ford, MM, was pastor. Sister M. Paul McKenna accompanied the sisters on this first trip, and they found work aplenty waiting them: a school for blind and crippled children, a creche for abandoned babies, a small dispensary, an old-folks' home, and the urgent language study. Already working at this mission were Sisters M. Rose Leifels, M. Lawrence Foley and M. Barbara Froehlich.

In mid-January 1923, the Maryknoll Sisters (Srs. M. Magdalen Doelger, M. Francis Davis, M. Rose Leifels, M. Lawrence Foley, M. Barbara Froehlich and M. Gertrude Moore) who had been in Yeungkong only two months experienced their first war scare. Following the advice of Father Ford, they bought extra supplies, dimmed their lights, and remained on the first floor of their convent, because they would have made good targets on the second and third floors.

Death of Mother Mary Joseph's Mother

Word of her mother's serious illness reached Mother Mary Joseph on the evening of February 11, 1923, the feast of Our Lady of Lourdes, just as she was about to give an illustrated talk to the sisters about Lourdes. She found that no train was available until after the talk was finished, so she decided to go ahead with it as planned.

Her sister Louise, Sister M. James, went off to get their things together. As Mother came to the front of the room to begin her talk, her face had the same repose that they saw in it daily. Her consistent response to moments of emergency, distress, or strain, was peaceful composure. Her face always seemed to reflect an inner peace and a confident hope that moved her to respond to the needs she encountered in life, even the most demanding. Her self-control was not the result of denial or repression, but rather a personal harmony composed of principles, emotions and habits, all based on a loving faith. *"Mother Mary Joseph was complete,"* said Sister Gemma Shea. *"She was never anything but noble in any situation, never less than herself."*

Mother and Sister James were with their mother for over a week before her death on February 20, 1923. Every visit which Mrs. Rogers had made to St. Teresa's had drawn the sisters closer to her. They loved to sit with her during their brief stretches of leisure time, to draw her out about home and family and Mollie, and to learn her own sane and solid views.

Death of Sister M. Gertrude Moore, R.N.

Known to the Chinese as *'Sister Doctor'* because of her total devotion to the sick, Sister Gertrude Moore had been among the sisters to arrive in Yeungkong, China, in November 1922. She fixed up a temporary dispensary on the compound of the rectory. A jolly, plump woman, the New York City nurse not only attended the crowded dispensary but went out to the villages on sick calls.

There was no doctor in the area, and in Sister Gertrude's first ten months at the mission she treated 6,000 cases of worms, blood poisoning, skin disease (leprosy) and eye afflictions. When a typhoid epidemic struck the town, she was treating fifty to one hundred patients daily until she herself contracted the disease from one of the boys at the school. She was due to renew her vows on August 4, but by then she was so ill she could not go to the chapel.

Sister Gertrude died on August 21, 1923, at the age of 28. Although she was not able to learn the local dialect in such a short time, her laughing eyes, smiling face and skillful care of the sick won her the love and respect of the population. News of Sister Gertrude's death inspired more young nurses to enter the Congregation.

Mother Mary Joseph's
First Mission Visitation, 1923-1924

Mother decided to accompany the third group of sisters to China in 1923, making her first official visit (referred to as a *Mission Visitation*). Before she left Maryknoll in September with the new group for China, Mother received a cable with the sad news that Sister Gertrude Moore had died of typhoid on August 21, 1923. Like Father Price who died in 1919, Sister Gertrude had lived for only a year in China before her death. Mother Mary Joseph's heart was filled with a sense of loss and compassion for her sisters. She immediately assigned another sister to join the group departing for China and included the priority of comforting the sisters and visiting Sister Gertrude's grave soon after her arrival in Yeungkong.

Mother and the assigned Sisters Dominic Guidera, Marie de Lourdes Bourguignon, Matthew Conlon, Miriam Schmitt, Patricia Coughlin and Ruth Riconda, with Richard Wenzel added to take the place of Gertrude Moore, left Maryknoll on September 11, 1923.

Mother departed for China from Seattle with eleven Maryknollers on the *SS President Jefferson,* September 23, 1923. With her were seven sisters, three priests, one auxiliary brother and Agnes Cogan, a younger sister of Maryknoll Sister Mary de Paul. Mother was relaxed, not worried about the oncoming storms nor preoccupied with the problems and challenges back home. She had four councilors who would shoulder such concerns and, in charge of the program for the formation of the novices was Sister Fidelia Delaney, OP, as competent and loveable as in her first year at Maryknoll.

On her way to China at last, Mother looked to the present, to those around her and their needs, and to the near future in China, where she would learn so much about the people and mission. The Maryknollers who traveled with her on this trip would recall how she soon became a focus of relationships and activities for the missioners and others who sought her out for greetings, information, suggestions, or just ordinary conversation.

Mother Mary Joseph's Letters and Diaries

The arrival of the *S.S. Jefferson* at Shanghai was a moving event for the missioners. They were now approaching the southern coast of China, and would soon be heading for their various destinations. The stories, letters, and diaries of Mother's first mission visitation to Asia in 1923-24 reflect her unique way of apostolic leadership, compassionate love and steadfast faith.

Her diary account of the journey (149 hand-written pages) and her letters both to Father Walsh and the sisters at Maryknoll were so vivid that it was possible to experience the events with her. In these narratives Mother's own words and actions and the stories, told by those with whom she traveled, reveal the depth of her warm personality and her loving outreach to others. She was spontaneously at home with her thoughts in the flow of the written word as in her spoken words.

Journey of Seven Months

This mission journey would be one of over seven months, during which Mother Mary Joseph would stop briefly in Japan (Yokohama and Kobe; later Shemoneseki and Kyoto) and visit many missions in Hong Kong, Macao and China (Shanghai, Canton, Pakkai, Kongmoon, Tai-Ho, Yeungkong, Chappo Hoiling, Ningpo, Chusan, Sam Shui, Wuchow, Hankow, Kaifeng, Chen Chow, Peking and Mukden). Mother's last stop would take her to Shingishu, Korea, where she and Sister Mary Paul would make their final vows as Maryknoll Sisters. This particular mission visitation made a deep and lasting impression on her, one she would later include in the list of the five most significant events of her life.

On the Junk to Yeungkong

Mother's comments in her *Diary* about the trip to Yeungkong on a junk revealed her ability to put hope and even joy into a difficult situation:

We reached the junk by sampan, climbed up the stairway let down for us and into the dirtiest boat you can imagine. Water, grease, vegetable skins, slime, and soldiers everywhere settling themselves for the night....Can you imagine me disappearing through a coal shuttle? Well, that's about what I did on the junk. We landed on the little platform before another jump introduced us into our cabin.

How can I picture it for you! Imagine a room about the size of our old office at St. Teresa's and less than two thirds as high; leave space enough to stand up in one corner and put a floor half-way up to the ceiling over the remainder. In the lower half was our baggage, our amahs and the catechist; on the floor of the upper section, were partitions about 6 inches high, dividing the space into six berths. At one end was a slightly raised shelf, with a window about 9 inches square. Two smaller openings gave us all the air we had; an oil lamp furnished light. Father Ford had a corner upstairs. In a similar section separated from us only by the platform below the deck were sick and wounded soldiers.

We could not stand up, so we squatted as best we could and ate our supper. Then we tried to settle ourselves. Sister Lawrence Foley and I had a shelf; one had the 'head' and the other the foot of each bed. We did not undress and the only thing between us and the boards were our shawls and the air pillows. We could not even sit up straight on our shelf, as we were so close to the beams. The place was infested with rats, enormous spiders and cockroaches and the night was punctuated by cries of distress when unwelcome visitors explored ears and faces. We said night prayers and sang every song we could recall ~ sacred and profane ~ and I believe we all got forty winks before morning.

Reality of Mission Life in the Orient

Mother's long hand-written letters indicated how completely she entered into the experience of mission life with her sisters, *"my own loved ones."* She discussed mission problems, worked with all the sisters on the Constitutions, visited their beginning works, and had a Chinese language lesson every day. She saw all of these activities important for herself. She wanted to know and appreciate the difficulties of mission life through her own experience rather than *"by merely hearing the matter discussed."* Nothing escaped her careful, personal concern.

In a letter to Father James A. Walsh, dated October 23, 1923,
Mother opened her heart, as she knew he would understand:

....Hitherto, I have, I realize now, viewed the whole mission life with the exaltation of the enthusiast, and I find myself appreciating for the first time, what perseverance in a vocation like ours entails. I look at these Sisters here, at my own loved ones, at our Priests and Brother Albert, with reverence and admiration. You, too, must have experienced similar situations on your visits, and can understand what is taking place in my heart and mind and soul these days....

Mother's Experience of Loneliness

Mother had the unique experience of a sense of loneliness,
the peculiar lot of every missioner. It remained vivid to her all her life:

I can remember so well the feeling that came over me during my first visit to Yeungkong. That visit had much in it that was novel in a new undertaking. It was a great adventure, and yet during the weeks I was there when I would be alone, there came over me an awful sense of loneliness, of being away from everything, a peculiar atmosphere that affected me more than anyone else at the time.

That is the kind of loneliness that overwhelmed our missioners. We know that the only thing that can overcome this loneliness is the Presence of God in the soul, the actual faith that God is with us, the realization of what God is to us. That is the important thing.

Unceasingly, Mother Mary Joseph spoke in one way or another of always living consciously in the Presence of God.

Visit to Sister Gertrude's Grave ~ 1923

On her arrival in Yeungkong, Mother went out with some of the sisters to visit Sister Gertrude's grave. Going out to the cemetery, they passed several moldering Chinese shrines before reaching an area barren of trees or grass which stretched away like a never-ending graveyard. The Christian cemetery could be distinguished from the rest by the cross that topped each tablet. Among other graves, Sister Gertrude's stood out. It was shallow and mounded like the rest, but the Maryknoll Fathers had a brick enclosure built around it to keep the earth from washing away. Mother thought gratefully of them when she saw it. She noticed how different people approached the grave, and even a leper who hid behind a bush. Mother was glad Sister Gertrude's grave was in that spot, so close to the lives of the poor whom she had served.

Father Ford's Appreciation of Mother Mary Joseph

While in Yeungkong, Mother had a number of contacts with Father Ford. It was observed that the Chinese were drawn to Mother like a magnet. Father Ford shared with those back home and he also had an article published in the July-August, 1924, issue of *The Field Afar* which sang his praises for Mother Mary Joseph's visit to the China Missions:

Mother Mary Joseph became one of the Chinese family, not a mere friend. She saw China from the inside of kitchens and of the family quarters, and smiled her way into the hearts of the womenfolk. She saw family life as we priests cannot see it....The women guiding boats or doing coolie's work would chat with her unreservedly, fully confident that she could divine their thoughts....She gathered the little girls about her and made them fearless in my presence. I always thought it was the foreign face and clothes that frightened them, but I look and dress more Chinese than the Reverend Mother did, and yet they ran to her and lost their bashfulness.

Father Ford saw in all this some significance for future mission work. Mother's whole trip emphasized the attraction our sisters will have on Chinese women, and this respect and love will bring forth mutual gifting of friendships through the years!

Final Vow Day in Korea ~ 1924

One of the high points of Mother's visit was making her final profession in Korea. Father Patrick Byrne met Mother and Sister M. Paul McKenna in Mukden, Manchuria, and brought them down into Korea. There, on February 11, 1924, on the Feast of Our Lady of Lourdes, in a tiny mud-walled house converted into a temporary chapel, Mother Mary Joseph and Sister Paul made their religious vows of poverty, chastity and obedience for life. Father Byrne heard their confessions in an absurd little room so crowded with two pieces of furniture that he could hardly sit and they could scarcely kneel.

Mother tried to communicate what she experienced to her Maryknoll Sisters but was content to leave the comprehension to their understanding hearts, and simply shared: *"There was nothing to distract....and everything to remind us of our obligations ~ poverty, chastity, obedience, foreign missions, sacrifice, restraint, souls."* Everything united them with the other Maryknoll Sisters across the world making these same life-long vows. On February 15, 1924, perpetual vows were taken by our sisters at Maryknoll-on-the-Hudson, Los Angeles and Seattle. The sisters in China made theirs on February 11, the same day as Mother and Sister Paul in Korea. Before the year 1924 was over, Mother would have established a mission in Loting, South China, in September, and another in Shingishu, Korea, in October.

First Woman to Enter from China: Sister M. Chanel Xavier

While working as a stenographer with Shell Oil Company in Hong Kong, Aurea Augusta Xavier read in the March 1920 issue of *The Field Afar* about the newly approved Religious Congregation, the Foreign Mission Sisters of St. Dominic. This prompted her to write Father James Anthony Walsh *"to inquire if this new order is for American girls only"* and also to express her *"very ardent desire to serve God and to join....for future missionary work in China."* She received a prompt reply from Mother Mary Joseph, together with the required application forms.

On June 25, 1923, Aurea joined Maryknoll as a postulant in Hong Kong. She came to the United States for her Novitiate, traveling with Mother Mary Joseph, arriving at Maryknoll, NY, three days before her formal Reception on April 19, 1924, receiving the name, Sister Mary Chanel. On April 30, 1926, she made her first profession, and three years later pronounced her final vows. In 1928 she was delighted to go to Hawaii to teach at the Maryknoll School in Punahou, Oahu. In 1931, she was assigned to Hong Kong, and for the next 44 years happily fulfilling the dream that drew her to Maryknoll: loving and serving God and the peoples of China, Hong Kong and Macau. She taught religion, art and music and also did nursing and catechetical work.

Sister Mary Chanel also taught in the local Novitiate in Kongmoon, China. She returned to the Center at Maryknoll, NY, in 1975, where her gift of music brought joy to many in the community either at liturgies or at recreation. Her artistic talent was also put to good use at our annual Bazaar. Sr. Mary Chanel returned to her Creator on July 31, 1987, with the usual tranquility and gentleness that characterized her whole life.

Sister Fidelia's Return to Sinsinawa

Mother arrived at Maryknoll, also, in time to experience the pangs of Sister Fidelia Delaney's leave-taking for Sinsinawa, Wisconsin. The greatest contribution that Sister Fidelia made was that she guided the development of Maryknoll Sisters in the pattern of Saint Dominic and she captured the spirit and purpose of Maryknoll. For this Mother Mary Joseph and her Maryknoll Sisters were ever grateful. On June 22, 1924, Mother took Sr. Fidelia's place as Novice Mistress pro-tem.

Reminiscing Over the Mission Experience

Reminiscing over the experiences of her recent trip, Mother Mary Joseph was convinced of the missioners' need for a strong spiritual and professional formation before going abroad. Such skills as nursing and teaching would enable the women to serve the people, but without an inner sense of God's presence, cultivating deep prayer, they could easily give in to fatigue, negativity and self-pity. One of her earliest ambitions was to establish a college where the sisters would receive a solid academic formation. This became a reality in 1931 with a three-year teacher training course, and later became a four-year college.

A Reflective Moment

Sr. Gertrude's life and death reflect Jesus who gave himself
into the hands of the disciples saying:
This is my body and I give it to you!
She witnesses to us the contemplative heart of our Maryknoll calling ~
to give ourselves wholeheartedly, as gift,
into the hands of one another and those we serve.

Resources

The above Reflections were adapted from:
Maryknoll's First Lady by Jeanne Marie Lyons, MM;
To the Uttermost Parts of the Earth by Camilla Kennedy, MM;
Maryknoll in China by Jean-Paul Wiest;
A Pictorial History by Sister Mary Francis Louise, MM;
Hearts on Fire by Penny Lernoux;
As One Lamp Lights Another by Barbara Hendricks, MM;
Mother Mary Joseph's Visitation Diaries, Section I, 11/23/23;
and *Maryknoll Mission Archives-Obituary of Sr. Mary Chanel Xavier.*

෨෦   ෨෦   ෨෦

#14 ~ Some Events from 1924 to 1929

Delegates to the 1st Maryknoll Sisters Chapter

Back Row: Sisters St. John Brown, Regina Reardon, Veronica Hartman, Columba Tarpey, MMJ, Felicita Clark, Teresa Sullivan, Marie Therese Kehoe. *Front Row:* Sisters Ambrose Crawford, Genevieve Beez, Gerard Gallagher, Mary de Paul Cogan, Margaret Mary Slattery, Lumena McMahon, Theophane Shea. *Delegates not pictured here were:* Sisters M. Gemma Shea, M. Aloysius McDonald, M. John Cahill.

The First Congregational Chapter in 1925

The first Canonical Visitation by His Eminence Cardinal Hayes was made on December 6, 1924. He decided that elections be held in the Spring of 1925, and the sisters' First Chapter took place in May 1925. The first most important task was electing officers to govern the congregation for the next six years. Among the 17 Sister-Delegates, there were voting proxies for those unable to attend (7 extra votes), making the total votes 24, representing 163 sisters. This was the first official canonical election of Mother Mary Joseph (MMJ) who was chosen unanimously as the first Mother General. The four Sister-Councilors elected were: Sisters M. Columba Tarpey, M. St. John Brown, M. de Paul Cogan, M. Felicita Clark and Sister M. Regina Reardon continued as Bursar General. MMJ was also to act as Local Superior. Sister M. Magdalen Doelger was recalled to Maryknoll from Yeungkong to be the Novice Mistress. This was the only Chapter that had voting by proxy. Sister M. de Paul Cogan, who was not a delegate, was elected to the Council and became the 18th delegate after the elections.

Discussions on Proposed Questions

After the elections, Mother convened the meeting to consider the proposed questions from the Chapter. The content included the care of the sick, the general discipline of the houses, language study – every effort to speak the native language, the vows, particularly obedience, the training of new members, and the means of financial support. Mother added her comments to the discussions on these subjects. She called attention to the fact that gradual changes were taking place both in the spiritual and material life of Maryknoll Sisters because *"we are growing."* Her balanced common sense prevailed always.

Mother stated a younger sister would be placed in authority because of her abilities, not on the basis of any seniority. She noted that charity is essential in the care of the sick. Having given some time to all questions, Mother and the sisters left unanswered some questions which only time could resolve when tested by experience.

Internment of Sisters Xavier Wholean and Emmanuel Donohue

An important event that occurred during the Chapter days was the bringing home of the remains of our dear Sisters M. Xavier Wholean, who died on February 19, 1917, and M. Emmanuel Donohue, a Novice, who was professed before she died on May 9, 1923 ~ both had been interred in St. Augustine Cemetery in Ossining. Sisters wearing mantles met the hearse as it entered the Maryknoll grounds and they followed in procession to a section for the sisters in the Society's cemetery plot, within sight of both Rosary House and the Seminary. Father James A. Walsh said the prayers at the graves. Then the sisters recited the *De Profundis,* as they filed past the graves, each one dropping a flower on the caskets.

First Assignments to Korea in 1924

Before leaving Korea at the time of her Mission Visitation, Mother had promised Father Patrick Byrne she would send sisters for the work there. The first assignments to Korea took place on June 23, 1924. The following were selected: Sisters Lucy Leduc, Juliana Bedier, Eugenia Gorman, Sylvester Collins, Andrew Smith and Augustine Kuper. They arrived in Gishu on October 21, 1924, a city of mud huts with straw roofs, or tile, if the owner was affluent. There was so much to get used to: the icy cold winter, difficulty of obtaining water, bread "imported" once a week, meat available every fifth day. The sisters also found the good that gave them joy in little events.

Their language teacher was Mrs. Helen Chang, wife of artist Louis Chang. His brother, John Chang, became South Korea's first Ambassador to Washington, and later Premier of Korea. His sister, Mary, was already in the Maryknoll Novitiate, and would become Sister Mary Agneta Chang. With her was Magdalena Kim, who became Sister Margaret Kim. Nakamura San, a former Buddhist and a teacher of Japanese to one of the sisters, was converted and four years later entered Maryknoll to become Sister M. Sabina Nakamura. These vocations later proved immensely valuable to the sisters' mission work in the Orient during World War II. As always, the sisters found their work ready and waiting for them: a dispensary was set up, an old-folks' home had already been established and catechetical work was begun.

Purchase of Bethany

In June 1924, the sisters purchased the 25-acre Clarke Estate in Ossining, where the main house had burnt down. This was the first property bought by the sisters. A new house was built and used as a Guest House. Father Walsh named it *Bethany*. Our sisters administered *Bethany* beginning November 21, 1925. In 1945, Bethany became a nursing residence for our sisters, and in 1956 a wing was added. In 1976, State approval was received to renovate the 4th floor of the Sisters' Center for a Residential Care Facility. In 1978, the Maryknoll Society purchased Bethany for the Mission Renewal Program, and eventually it became home to the Maryknoll Lay Missioners till they moved to the Walsh Building on the Maryknoll Society Compound in 2013.

Preparations for the Motherhouse

During the middle twenties, Mother Mary Joseph (MMJ) began planning for a Motherhouse. Soon the last little frame buildings on the property would be full. She watched on a February day in 1926 the sisters plowing through snow drifts to Mass and prayers in one house, to work in another, to meals in another. She saw their sopping skirts while they stood outside the different houses knocking the snow off their rubbers. She thought of their crowded dormitories where one could just stand between the beds, and of the beds that had taken over the community room in St. Joseph's, as well as beds being put at the end of the hallways and at the head of staircases.

She thought of the young women writing to her to inquire about becoming Maryknoll Sisters, and she felt that the time had come to do something. She set herself to increase the income in every way compatible with the life and purpose of the Community ~ selling sisters' handiwork, setting up a stamp department, making greeting cards, initiating an electroplating department and other initiatives. These efforts helped but did not suffice. MMJ made an appeal to the Catholic Daughters of America who pledged themselves generously to assist us. The results could not approximate what was required.

New Initiatives for Securing Funds

With a sense of urgency, Mother picked up her pen and wrote to Cardinal Dougherty of Philadelphia. *"Where pastors were willing, might her sisters stand at the door of the churches of his Archdiocese and receive the offerings of the parishioners?"* Promptly, and to many surprisingly, Cardinal Dougherty answered, *"Yes."* Later, when approached, Archbishop Glennon of St. Louis and Cardinal Hayes of New York gave the same permission. This was the beginning of our Development Department! Mission Circles were formed by women friends of the sisters, and every month they sent small checks to help support the missioners and finance the Motherhouse.

Although the well-to-do and famous helped, including Shirley Temple who turned up at a Tea Party, most contributors were working-class Catholics who went without lunch or walked to work for a week to send a few dollars. Children saved pennies and nickels to give to the Maryknoll mite boxes, and many families sent bags of cancelled stamps to be sold. *The Field Afar* frequently solicited funds for the construction of the Motherhouse. On September 1, 1929, ground was broken for the Motherhouse across the street from the Society Seminary.

Building Community

For Mother and her sisters, mission constituted every aspect of their lives together. Mission was the way of life. While engaged in the long-range planning demanded for the building of a Motherhouse, Mother was forming in another and more important way a community, which reflected a family spirit. She arranged a series of classes entitled, *Morning Talks for Benjamins,* directed to the new members. She carefully shaped the Maryknoll spirit through the conferences she gave and circulated throughout the congregation; through the wide variety of books she provided in the library for private reading and during reading at meals; and through her personal outreach to build relationships with her sisters. Often reading during meals was selected from books and articles by missionaries.

Her own accessibility was constant ~ all leading the Community to a greater and deeper sense of family and mission. She was open to adaptations in community life and in prayer, leading to the formation of her sisters as true religious and missioners. She was making choices, too, among the many fields and works now held out to her sisters that benefited the most needy in our world.

Mother Mary Joseph's Second Mission Visitation

In October 1926, Mother set out on her second mission visitation to Asia. She had already appointed Sister Paul McKenna to be Mission Superior of the sisters in China, responsible for the development and direction of the missions. Things were going well for her sisters in China, but there were some problems in Korea which she had to handle while in Asia. During this mission visitation Mother committed her community to work in the Philippines. In January 1926, the first group of sisters had already arrived in Manila: Sisters Teresita O'Donnell, Philip Bergeron, Mary de Sales Mullen, de Chantal Galligan and Assumpta Duffy and in June they began a school in Malabon, Philipppines. In July, Sisters Theodore Farley, Angela Dalton and Caritas McCabe arrived.

When on her visitation, Mother committed more sisters to work in the Philippines. She realized that a mission superior of outstanding character was needed for the program projected there. Writing to Father James A. Walsh in January 1927, from Kowloon, China, after visiting the Philippines, she first outlined the circumstances of the new work to be undertaken. She then shared:

> *I can hear you gasp when I mention it, but I would like very much to have Sister Columba launch this new and very important work. There are strong objections, of course, to sister's leaving the Motherhouse. As first councilor, we would have to get permission for a year's leave of absence. She is needed at Maryknoll and no one can quite fill her place. But I believe there is a greater need here for the moment.*

By 1927, the Maryknoll Sisters were in Manila taking over St. Paul's Hospital which included a school to train nurses, and St. Mary's Residence Hall, a hostel for Catholic students attending the Philippine Normal School and the University of the Philippines. Sister Columba Tarpey was assigned the Mission Superior in the Philippines, arriving there in April 1928.

Hawaii

A new mission venture was taking place in Hawaii, the crossroads of the Pacific. Maryknoll's Father Kress had invited the sisters to staff his new school in Sacred Heart Parish in Honolulu. The sisters arrived in September 1927. Four days later the grade school opened with 93 boys and 77 girls.

Sister Veronica Hartman was Mission Superior, and with her were Sisters Berchmans Flynn, Immaculata Brennan, Matthias Lickteig, Robert Rust and Tarcisius Doherty. Those missioned to Heeia were Sisters Alphonsa Bergeron, Gregory Mackey, Pieta Kirby and Adrienne Mundy.

Education of the Sisters

Mother had begun to continue the education of at least some of her sisters for various needs in the missions as early as she could and with the generous help of such communities as the Religious of the Sacred Heart at Manhattanville, the Mount St. Vincent Sisters of Charity, and the Seattle Sisters of Providence. In 1926, she was able to open a house near the Catholic University of America until a training school for teachers could be initiated for her sisters.

The Tompkins Property

In June 1927, the Maryknoll Society purchased the Tompkins' Estate across the way from their present property, which extended from the highest point in Westchester to Brookside Lane. On August 15, Father Walsh blessed the family dwelling on the highest point naming it *Regina Coeli*. This became part of the Sisters' Novitiate. On November 7, 1928, the Maryknoll Sisters purchased from the Society 53 acres of the former Tompkins' property, including *Regina Coeli* hilltop, and the land on which the Sisters Center would be built. The Society retained the southern portion of 8.86 acres. In July 1945, on our inquiry of the Society to purchase this remaining portion, they made a gift of it to us, in lieu of the work of the sisters through the years. In the 1970's, the Society bought from us the small piece of land and house on Brookside Lane and Ryder Road.

The Depression

In October 1929, the nation's economy suddenly crashed. Just a month before, ground had been broken for the new Motherhouse. Hence, it was principally through prayer, and perhaps a genuine miracle, that the contract for construction was signed on May 1, 1930. For less than a month after the crash, stocks declined 40 percent, and as the new year wore on, banks and factories closed, businesses failed, mills and mines shut down all over the country. At Maryknoll, as elsewhere, the sharp pinch was felt. Many who used to give could do so no longer. To ask to collect at church doors became impossible, since church-goers were on relief themselves or helping friends and relatives who were. Loans had been secured, a first and then a second mortgage on the Motherhouse raised. Each time the interest came due on one or the other, it seemed impossible that it could be paid. Sometimes an unexpected gift or legacy received only the day before would make it possible. Bills stacked up. "*What are we going to do, Mother*," one of the sisters asked. "*Don't worry, sister,*" Mother said in her most equable tones, "*this is God's work. God will take care of it.*"

A Reflective Moment

Wisdom is trusting God unconditionally!

Resources

The above Reflections were adapted from:
Maryknoll's First Lady by Jeanne Marie Lyons, MM;
To the Uttermost Parts of the Earth by Camilla Kennedy, MM;
Hearts on Fire by Penny Lernoux;
Maryknoll Sisters, A Pictorial History by Sister Mary Francis Louise, MM;
1925 Distaff (Sisters Diary) by Eunice Tolan, MM, and Incarnata Farrelly, MM.

જી જી જી

Maryknoll Sisters
1912 ~ 2012

©

Making God's Love Visible

#15 ~ The Maryknoll Spirit

**Mother Mary Joseph on August 4, 1930,
gave her first reflective formulation on the
'Maryknoll Spirit,' which was a key
to all her later reflections on its meaning.
We share some excerpts from this conference:**

*"As one lamp lights another nor grows less,
so nobleness enkindles nobleness."*
From the Poem *Yussouf* by James Russell Lowell

We can easily see the meaning of these words. We know that if we take a candle and light another one, the light of the first does not lessen, rather it gives light to the second one. And so it is with us, with our virtues. Kindness begets kindness and charity begets charity, and the first act does not grow less, rather it has increased. If we could only be conscious that every act of kindness will beget another act of kindness, and an act of charity will bring another act of charity, how little trouble we would have in life.

Now all of this applies to our life as Maryknoll Sisters and the spirit of our congregation depends very much upon the application of those very words, *"As one lamp lights another nor grows less, so nobleness enkindles nobleness."* We know every community has its own distinctive spirit, and we hear a great deal about the *Maryknoll Spirit*. Those of us who have been here from the beginning have seen people come to Maryknoll, who had in mind that they would see something here that had been very much exaggerated, that a lot of the talk that they had heard about Maryknoll was really publicity.

But thanks to God, like the scoffer who went to church to laugh and remained to pray, so many who have come prepared to be indulgently kind to Maryknoll, have remained and gone away admiring the special gift of God to us, which is our spirit. A spirit is something that is intangible and it is hard to describe. Now what is the *Maryknoll Spirit*:

➤ I only know that I like to feel that people see in us real simplicity, that guilelessness of which Jesus spoke when He saw Nathaniel approach Him, *Behold a person without guile* ~ no subterfuge, no hypocrisy.

➤ I like to feel that people see reflected in our eyes the charity of Christ, and on our lips the words that speak of the charity of Christ; that they find our ears filled with the charity of Christ and closed to gossip and scandal, but ever sympathetic to the grief and sorrows of others.

➤ I like to feel that they see in us the spirit of mutual love and tenderness which certainly existed in the early ages of the Church when the non-Christians said, *"See how they love one another."*

We have tried from the beginning to cultivate a spirit which is extremely difficult and which for a long time might have been misunderstood even by those who were nearest to us. That spirit is the retention of our own natural dispositions, the retention of our own individuality, having in mind of course that all of these things need to be corrected where radically wrong, and all of them supernaturalized. I say it is a most difficult spirit that we have chosen for ourselves.

After all, it is not so difficult to settle upon a particular type which you would wish your sisters to resemble, marking out certain observances, certain postures, certain poses, and you can cut every sister out according to a pattern or, rather, you can pour her into a mold and have her turn out marked with the outlines desired. But for us, that sort of development will hardly do.

We expect to go out and live among those who may be suspicious of us, who may not like us, who may respect us only when we have proven our virtue, our sincerity and our usefulness to them. And for this we need all our individuality, all our generosity, all our graciousness and sweetness and simplicity, all our powers of gentle persuasiveness. In fact, we need all of the things which the good God has given to us. And each one of us, in her own work, with her own particular attractiveness, is to be used by God as a particular tool to do a particular work and to be present to particular people. How sincerely then should we lend ourselves to this sanctifying of our own natural qualities; and how easy it is to explain it to others when we ourselves understand it.

Now what are some of the qualities that our experience tells us are necessary to fulfill our Maryknoll vocation? What should we be if we are going to make those about us happy? It is a good thing to keep in mind the word 'others.' How do I affect others, what can I do for others, how can I help others, how can I see the grief of others? Think always of others and you will not have time to think of yourself. You will come upon one of the necessary characteristics – generosity. There can be no Maryknoll Sister, no missionary worthy of the name, that is not heroically generous, generous to the very last inch of her being, generous in the giving of her time, of her talents, generous in her thoughts, generous in every possible phase of life. I share a passage from a letter which one of our sisters wrote:

> *As yet I have suffered no ill effect from the climate. There is only one fever I dread, the S.P., or self-pity bacillus. From my short mission experience, I have become conscious that self-pity and lack of generosity are the most destructive germs that can enter a missioner's soul.*

The longer you live, the more is your generosity going to be called upon.
Mother Mary Joseph - 1930

Try to make it a rule that in all things which are not of vital importance, that you yield. You know it takes strength to yield. Of course if you yield just for the sake of avoiding a scene where there is a matter of justice involved, then you are wrong, but in other matters always be the one who is ready to yield to another. How much happiness it will give you! It is like oil in a machine; things will run so much smoother if you keep this in mind.

There is another trait which I think is most important for a missioner, almost a sister virtue to cooperation, and we call it adaptability. Adaptability is that power of creating anywhere that we may be sent the feeling of fitting in, and of attempting anything which you are asked to do. You will always find that you are going to be moved about from this work to that, from one house to another, from one room to another. It just seems to be part of our life. If we allow ourselves to go on inwardly rebelling against these changes, inwardly wishing that this might not be so, boiling, seething inside, then we are going to ruin our minds as well as our bodies. We need to train ourselves to go up or down, in or out, with this person or that, in any work whatsoever and still try to the very best of our ability to accept these changes.

If we school ourselves in the way of the 'Maryknoll Spirit,' God can work miracles through our hands.
Mother Mary Joseph - 1930

Excerpts from 'Hearts on Fire,'
Centenary Edition, Orbis Books, 2012

One hundred years ago, the small band of women who came to Hawthorne, NY, dreamed with audacious hope of spreading, preaching and witnessing to the mission of Jesus to the ends of the earth. They created a life in community that utterly relied on God's providence. That hope, in the loving providence of God, gained depth, courage and meaning with the realization that the world they vowed to serve also called for an ongoing conversion and transformation.

Over the years we, Maryknoll Sisters, have immersed ourselves in cultures and with peoples, governments and geography totally different from our own. We have also continued to experience a God who is always with us, and the awesome surprise that God also waits for us in these landscapes of life into which we are sent. Again and again, we encounter other dreamers in search of the sacred and the quest for meaning. On this road, we join our sisters and brothers on a pilgrimage to engage in God's emerging dream through Jesus.

Today we are ready to begin our second century of mission with nearly 500 Maryknoll Sisters already in position in and for a globalized world. We have been blessed and hold promise for our church and world! We welcome the future, nurtured by the past. The fire and passion for mission continues to burn steadily within out hearts, lit long ago deep in our souls. So we recall a blessing by our Founder, Mother Mary Joseph, some 75 years ago on our 25th Anniversary, January 6, 1937:

And so tonight I thought we would drink a little toast to our past,
particularly in thanksgiving for all that God has given to us ~
to the blessed memories of the past,
whether painful or pleasant ones ~
and to our future, to hope that God's blessings
will rest upon us and that each and every one of us,
individuals, and we, as a Community,
will respond fully to the graces that God will give us.

Mother Mary Joseph
Silver Jubilee ~ January 6, 1937

Janice McLaughlin, MM, ends
'Hearts on Fire' with the words:

Our 100 years have taught us the incredible diversity and richness of cultures and the need to preserve them from extinction. It has also taught us that the message of Jesus is as relevant as ever. In the words of our Founder, Mother Mary Joseph:

The dominant factor in our lives is love,
love of God and love of neighbor.

She described our spirit as being
'a reflection of the love of God.'

Our numbers are fewer and our nationalities more varied but we seek to be faithful to her vision and we look forward to the future with hope. Our Founder's words to one of the pioneer women sum up the attitude that will usher us into the next 100 years:

Let's just go together and see
what God has in store for us!
Mollie Rogers (MMJ) to Margaret Shea (Sr. Gemma) in 1912

A Reflective Moment
Let us give ourselves to grateful prayer for
the Gift of Maryknoll. For we are blessed by
God's Spirit and empowered by Mother Mary Joseph
and companions willing to walk
uncharted paths into the future!

Resources
The above Reflections were adapted from:
To the Uttermost Parts of the Earth
by Camilla Kennedy, MM, p. 207 ff., and
Hearts on Fire, Centenary Edition, pp. 290-201, 301.

80   80   80

#16 ~ General Chapter 1931

Sitting: Sisters Beata Mackie. Pauline Lebeau, Theodore Farley, Martina Bridgeman, Regina Reardon, Genevieve Beez, Caritas McCabe, Clement Quinn, Gerard Gallagher, Raymund Carpenter;
Standing: Sisters M. de Paul Cogan, Aloysius McDonald, Coronata Sheehan, Marie Therese Kehoe, Veronica Hartman, Columba Tarpey, Mother Mary Joseph Rogers, Sisters St. Teresa Hayden, Andrew Smith, Edward Diener, Felicita Clarke, Paul McKenna, Magdalen Doelger and Jude Babione.

Our First Constitutions

The preparation for the Second General Chapter of the Congregation, to be held in 1931, included work toward an approval of the draft of the first Constitutions. Mother Mary Joseph who had made two extended visitations to the sisters laboring in the mission fields knew from experience what had been felt almost from the beginning. The nature of a vocation to mission work demanded something different from the generally accepted religious manner. To be a religious missioner demanded, in her words, *"the sanctifying of one's natural qualities."* To reflect this understanding in the precise canonical language of the Constitutions took great effort.

Based on an analysis of her experience, Mother outlined the difficulties of the sisters' mission work: language acquirement, social conditions of women, lack of definite work plans and financial support, and climatic stresses. Envisioning the sisters more directed to catechetical work and direct evangelization, she indicated their need of experience and training in the same measure that they are required for priests. A long time had been spent in work on the first Constitutions both by Mother and her Sister-Councilors. In order to incorporate the things peculiar to the Maryknoll Sisters, they added those matters which they had in mind as a result of mission work. They carefully went over every paragraph and prepared a copy for each Sister-Delegate to the 1931 Second General Chapter.

Maryknoll Teacher Training School

In 1931, Mother began another long-range project, arranging for Sister Mary de Paul Cogan to begin a teacher training school when the Motherhouse was completed. Mother had always encouraged educational enrichment for all her sisters and had provided various courses whenever opportunities arose.

Now Maryknoll Teacher Training School would be set up with a three-year course. This would develop in later years into Maryknoll Teachers College with a fully accredited four-year course leading to a Bachelor in Education Degree. Meanwhile other communities continued their generosity in providing additional opportunities for our sisters to continue their studies.

Excerpt of Talk by Mother Mary Joseph for Opening of 1931 Chapter Assembly

July 9, 1931 was the opening day of the Second General Chapter. The Delegates were: Sisters Beata Mackie, Pauline Lebeau, Columba Tarpey, Theodore Farley, Martina Bridgeman, Regina Reardon, Gerard Gallagher, Genevieve Beez, Coronata Sheehan, Caritas McCabe, Clement Quinn, Aloysius McDonald, Raymond Carpenter, dePaul Cogan, Marie Therese Kehoe, Veronica Hartman, St. Teresa Hayden, Andrew Smith, Edward Diener, Felicita Clarke, Paul McKenna, Magdalen Doelger, Jude Babione and Mother Mary Joseph who set the tone for the opening of the Second General Chapter.

We want to feel that everything about this Chapter bears the impress of the Hand of God. We have prepared a financial report of the community, and a spiritual report covering the six years. It has been gratifying to note the progress that has been made in every direction. We should all remember, and especially the delegates at a time like this, that into your hands the communities you represent have entrusted their well-being and good name and family confidence.

We need your prayers particularly for the elections. What they are going to be, we do not know. We have had no discussions of them as far as I know, although tomorrow afternoon when the report is being discussed, the sisters are quite free to discuss among themselves the candidates eligible for the various offices.

Details Concerning Auxiliary Bishop Dunn's Arrival and Congregational Elections

Mother shared: "*Bishop Dunn is coming tomorrow night and we expect to have Mass for the entire community in St. Martha's at 6:45 on Saturday morning, July 11. It is likely that Bishop Dunn will give his exhortation to the Community at that time. At 8:30 a.m., the formal elections will begin, with a prayer to the Holy Spirit in the Chapel here. At the end of the elections, when the last officer has been elected and the Bishop has announced the elections to the delegates, all the sisters should be ready to be assembled in the chapel.*"

Gratitude for Sisters' Cooperation ~
Local Superior at the Motherhouse

Mother expressed her gratitude: *"I take this occasion to thank all the Sisters for the cooperation they have given in the past six years. They have been difficult years in many ways, and yet years that were filled with happiness and consolation. And I would like to thank especially the councilors who have worked so faithfully and untiringly with me. One thing we will have, after the General Chapter, will be a Local Prioress. We will have not only the General Government, but there will be here at the Center a Local Superior with her Council, acting independently of the Central Government, just as any other local house does. We will have much to pray for ~ not only the question of elections but the assignments which must come after it and the many changes which will be brought about once the Constitutions are established."*

Results of the Elections

Saturday, July 11, brought the good news that the delegates to the General Chapter re-elected Mother Mary Joseph as Mother General for a second six-year term.

Also elected were:

Sr. Columba Tarpey as 1st Councilor;

Sr. Mary de Paul Cogan as 2nd Councilor and Secretary General;

Sr. M. Veronica Hartman as 3rd Councilor;

Sr. M. St. Teresa Hayden as 4th Councilor;

Sr. Regina Reardon as Treasurer General

Because of the hot weather, many sessions were held under one of the large trees or at Regina Coeli. Moreover, except for the Chapel and interior decorations, the Motherhouse provided space for the General Chapter Delegates to hold its final meeting there. The building was not completely finished until 1932.

Excerpt of Mother Mary Joseph's Talk on the Chapter

The Chapter was a great joy to all of us. The delegates brought to it a most intelligent cooperation. All of those who were present felt that God blessed us and blessed you in some special way. Most of the things appear in the Constitutions; therefore, we will not discuss them now. I intend to take them as soon as the Sisters have a copy of the Constitutions and make spiritual reading from them for fifteen minutes a day with you, discussing the matters, so that in going over them together we will have a like understanding of all that is in them.

The preparation of the new Constitutions will be of interest to all of you. We had been working on it for a long time, and when I went to Rome last year with Sister Paul (McKenna) and Sister Eunice (Tolan), Father Nolan, OP, gave us a scheme in Latin which is being used by the Congregation of Religious, 90% of which is common to all communities, allowing 10% for the incorporation of things peculiar to each community. This I worked on myself comparing it with our own Constitutions.

Mother Mary Joseph Shares Directives from the Chapter

Regarding the Mantle: "*We chose to have for Chapel use, a black cappa, a regular Chapel mantle. We would like eventually to get the real Dominican religious mantle used exclusively in the Chapel or for processions.*"

Divine Office: "*Another matter brought up was that, if it proved to be practical and did not take up more time than our present prayers plus our present Office, that we should substitute the Divine Office for the Little Office of the Blessed Virgin. This is the growing spirit of the Church. A group will try this out. Our purpose is not to try to take up anything difficult for the Sisters or which will make the daily life any more crowded than it is now. If we find it feasible, we shall work it out in the community.*"

Regions: "*For the purpose of facilitating our government, we have decided to divide the sections in which our Sisters work into Regions. This will be geographically settled upon by the General Council.*"

Community Medal: "*We shall have a community medal to replace the mission medal. On one side will be the Annunciation, and on the other side the shield of the Maryknoll Society with the motto, Ecce Ancilla Domini.*"

White Habit: The white habit was adopted by a vote of 23 to 1, for the entire community. (However, at the 1937 Chapter, the color of the habit reverted back to gray, while the white habit would be worn in the tropics.)

Appointments for the Motherhouse
by Mother and her Council

Sr. Felicita Clarke as Local Superior
Sr. Loyola Vollet as 1st Councilor
Sr. Mark Killoran as Local Bursar
Sr. Miriam Dolores Latham as Directress of Postulants
Sr. Theophane Shea as Procurator General
Srs. Luke Logue and Ambrose Crawford as Local Procurators

New Regions and Regional Superiors

1. South China ~ Sr. Paul McKenna;
2. Korea-Manchuria ~ Sr. Genevieve Beez;
3. Philippines ~ Sr. Trinita Logue;
4. Hawaii ~ Sr. Tarsicius Doherty.

The Contemplative Community

On August 30, 1931, Mother Mary Joseph gave a talk on the decisions of the 1931 General Assembly, among them the approval of a Cloister (now known as the Contemplative Community) within Maryknoll. Mother shared:

One of the most important things which we decided was the final settlement upon what many of the Sisters may have expected, and which some have known about for a long time, the contemplative branch of our community. We have had this branch in mind since the beginning of our work in 1914. We have never departed from the idea....In 1914, I went to Rome with Miss Ward. While there, we went to the Convent of the Blue Nuns, Nursing English Sisters. While there I saw these Sisters at the altar constantly and I was told that they always have two Sisters praying for the other Sisters whose work is visiting and care of the poor and rich sick in their homes. And there was born the idea of a contemplative branch for Maryknoll. While we were in Rome last year (1930), I spoke to Father Nolan, O.P., who said, It is the final stamp of the approval of God upon the work that the Maryknoll Sisters are doing.

Training of Native Sisterhoods

The first Rule (#14 Constitution) of the Catholic Foreign Mission Society of America, approved by Pope Benedict XV on July 15, 1915, had called for the Maryknoll Society *"to form at the earliest opportunity a native clergy as the most efficacious means of perpetuating its works of conversion."* The Maryknoll Sisters were equally convinced of the importance of building up an indigenous Church by forming native sisterhoods and training catechists, by stimulating the laity to apostolic activity and by founding Christian institutions.

Their first Constitution called for cooperation with the priests and brothers and by 1931, their Constitution explicitly identified *"the training of native sisterhoods"* as a priority of the sisters' mission activity. Among the twenty foreign mission centers established by Mother Mary Joseph and her sisters during the 1930's in Asia and the Hawaiian Islands, six native novitiates were initiated. There were four in South China (Kongmoon, 1926; Kaying, 1930; Wuchow, 1938; Kweilen, 1939); one in Manchuria, 1931; and one in Korea, 1932.

The Maryknoll Movement
As of January 1, 1931, we had:
292 Professed Sisters; 70 Novices; 53 Postulants

The number of sisters continued to increase. Those at Maryknoll, NY, still lived in six dwellings on the Maryknoll Society's compound ~ some in St. Teresa's and Rosary House, others in St. Michael's, St. Joseph's and Regina Coeli, and some even in two dormitories above *The Field Afar* offices. The Professed Sisters had a Chapel in Rosary House, so the novitiate could use St. Martha's Chapel. The sisters were eagerly looking forward to the completion of the Motherhouse and their moving in, which actually happened in March 1932. The Maryknoll Movement continued in every direction during the next decade!

Mission Houses
From 1925 through 1934 twenty new mission houses were opened overseas by the Maryknoll Sisters: four in China, two in Korea, four in Manchuria, four in the Philippine Islands and six in the Hawaiian Islands. Two problems which arose from this rapid development of the Asian and Pacific missions were inevitable: inadequate preparation of the sisters and lack of experienced leadership. Mother recognized this situation and carefully chose those sisters who appeared to have the qualities needed for leadership both overseas and at home. Mother did her best to foster leadership among the sisters, sharing her responsibilities as widely as possible.

Prayer Life Enriched
Mother Mary Joseph, who was gifted musically, sought out the latest teaching on church liturgy, including use of the missal and eventually the daily recitation of the Divine Office. In the 1920's and early 1930's small groups of Maryknoll Sisters studied church music at Pius X School of Liturgical Music, Manhattanville, NY, during the academic season. A group of sisters would study at Pius X each summer, and teachers from Pius X would come weekly to Maryknoll to give classes.

The prayer life of the Teresians had been woven into the daily schedule of work and recreation as planned by Father Walsh, who from the beginning held up Teresa of Avila as their model. In addition to Teresa of Avila, saints with the strongest influence in the early years were the Blessed Virgin Mary and St. Joseph.

In the decade of the 1920's, the Dominican Saints, Dominic and Catherine of Siena became a part of the Maryknoll Sisters' heritage. It was at that time that Mother Mary Joseph became strongly attracted to the women mystics of the medieval period, in particular Teresa of Avila, Catherine of Siena and Gertrude of Helfta. In her conferences Mother often referred to these women saints as models for the sisters' life of prayer.

Father James A. Walsh and the Apostolic Delegate

Father James A. Walsh was invited to speak at the 1931 Chapter. He stressed that we need to prepare for the next generation; keep in mind that you are working for tomorrow...for the day when you will have disappeared and need to lay your foundations now in view of that future. He congratulated us on the building of the Motherhouse and said that the Apostolic Delegate visited the nearly finished Motherhouse and was very much impressed. He said he saw not only a building, but an *"aedificatio ~ a building which typified a spirit."* That is what impressed him!

A Reflective Moment

On January 2, 1947, Mother Mary Joseph said:

We began with nothing....
God accomplished this wonder of Maryknoll!

Resources

The above Reflections were adapted from:
To the Uttermost Parts of the Earth by Camilla Kennedy, MM;
Maryknoll Sisters, A Pictorial History by Sister Mary Francis Louise, MM;
1931 *Distaff (Sisters Diary)* by Eunice Tolan, MM, and Incarnata Farrelly, MM;
As One Lamp Lights Another by Barbara Hendricks, MM.

ಏ ಏ ಏ

#17 ~ Some Events from 1931 to 1932

Auxiliary Bishop Dunn and Yankee Stadium

In the fall of 1931, Bishop Dunn, Auxiliary of the New York Archdiocese, who knew how fragile the community's finances stood, made a suggestion to Mother Mary Joseph: *"People able to attend baseball games must surely have something to give away. Why not have the sisters collect at Yankee Stadium?"* To collect at Yankee Stadium would be quite unique, and Mother followed through on the suggestion. On a brisk Fall afternoon Maryknoll Sisters stood outside the Stadium holding baskets and watching the thousands who poured out through the wide gates. Afterwards, when they pooled what they had received, they had exactly $31.86 in nickels and pennies!

March 2, 1932 ~ Move to the Motherhouse

The day of moving into the Motherhouse was March 2, 1932. Mother, her Council and Sister M. Felicita Clarke, the first Motherhouse Superior, moved over a week earlier. All day on March first, the sisters packed, sorted and crated at one side of the road, and unpacked, unsorted and uncrated at the other. The seminarians had a 'free' day to help with the moving. Father General blessed the sisters, reminding them to thank God for the generous blessings bestowed upon them and to pray gratefully for the many American families whose sacrifices in those hard depression days had made this new home possible. The sisters from seven scattered dwellings moved into the Motherhouse. The next day there was a huge snowstorm with the water power failing. Until they could arrange for an increased supply, even dishwashing had to be scheduled.

Sister Felicita got so accustomed to reckoning gallons that she inadvertently ordered fifty gallons of ice cream (instead of quarts)! When the dealer quoted the price, Sister was astonished and canceled the order, saying they could not afford it.

The dealer called back to ask if she really wanted fifty gallons! Sister explained her preoccupation and then ordered fifty quarts of ice cream at a reasonable price. The event of the sisters' moving was experienced as a moment of separation ~ a crossing over the road from the familiar Maryknoll Seminary grounds to all the unfamiliar paths of one large *new home*. It was also a very emotional experience.

Mother Mary Joseph's Meditation - March 3, 1932

Mother's morning meditation on March 3 marked the moving *"as a very final step towards a new phase of life."* She exhorted the sisters to look with gratitude upon their new house as a place to better fulfill their common mission vocation: *"So today, while we know that under God through the providence of the poor who have helped us, we are going into a new home which we have built ourselves, we must not lose sight of the fact that even that which is apparently so much our own would not have been possible had we not the Society fostering us, guiding us. The protection of Father General (Father James A. Walsh) has been to us like the visible sign of the protecting Hand of God."*

While Mother experienced joy and satisfaction in the clearer self-identity their own Motherhouse would give the sisters, she was also concerned that this distancing from the Maryknoll Priests and Brothers might cause the sisters to forget all that had been given to them by the Society since the beginnings at Hawthorne in 1912.

Natural Process of Maturing

The move to the Motherhouse was a separation experienced also as a natural process of maturing. It was reflected most at work in a growth toward independence ~ both by the Maryknoll Sisters and the Maryknoll Fathers and Brothers.

On the one hand, Mother found there was less consultation between herself and Father Walsh, *"a natural effect of growth"* in all areas. On the other hand, all the Maryknoll Sisters considered themselves daughters in Christ of Father Walsh. Yet in the passage of years, each had moved in a direction which determined its own distinctive historical development. The sisters had become missioners who expressed their vocation through religious life. Within this context of being religious missioners, Mother was forming the sisters in a uniqueness that was all our own as Maryknoll Sisters.

Great Depression

The devastating effects of the Great Depression tempered Mother Mary Joseph's sense of accomplishment. In a letter to Dominican Sister Fidelia Delaney, who remained a close friend, she described the months that followed the move to the Motherhouse as extraordinarily difficult. *"Unless help comes from some supernatural source, I do not know what we shall do, for our income is cut off almost entirely by the depression outside. Still God has sustained us in a most striking way through the years, and I cannot feel that anything untoward will happen now."*

The Motherhouse Compound

Compared with the Maryknoll Society's compound in the 1930's, the Motherhouse grounds were a veritable wilderness. For many years the barest work could be done on it, until during the war in the 1940's the United States Government released the interned Japanese rock and landscape artist, Mr. Ryozo Peter Kado. After his release, Mr. Kado and his family spent several years at Maryknoll, where his exquisite, patient and detailed work, especially his masterpiece replica of the Lourdes Grotto, made the sisters' grounds awesome. Mr. Kado found the stones for the Grotto on the property. They were not cemented but fitted together artistically and scientifically, and support each other by their own weight.

The College of Cleaners

Around the time of the moving, a group of Novices were completing their canonical year. They had spent their mornings cleaning up the post-construction debris. They dubbed themselves *The College of Cleaners* and rounding out the year, held a mock graduation, to which they invited Mother Mary Joseph. She came, bearing a bouquet of new dish mops, and amid laughter and applause, took her place. The college song composed for the occasion was sung, and she then conferred the degrees which had been listed for her to award:

To Sister Stella Marie, the degree of D.D.M., Doctor of Dry Mopping;
To Sister Miriam de Lourdes, the degree of PH.D., Doctor of Phine Dusting,
and so forth....

At cries for *"Speech, Speech,"*
Mother launched into an impromptu commencement address!

Maryknoll Teacher Training School

October 12, 1931, the Teacher Training School opened with classes held at Rosary House and at the Chalet. Sister Mary de Paul Cogan was the Dean, with the following teachers and classes:

Sr. Lumena McMahon ~ History of Civilization,
Geography, Written Expression
Sr. Christopher Naumann ~ History of Education
Sr. Corde Lorang ~ Arithmetic
Sr. Jeanne Marie Lyons ~ Religion Methods
Sr. Maria Regis Murphy ~ Health Education

(Outside Teachers)
Fr. Thomann ~ Psychology
Fr. Lane ~ Character Training

The first students were: Sisters Marie Rosaire Greaney, Berchmans Flynn, Cordula Vonfeldt, Rose Carmel Reilly, Ann Francis McCoy and Candida Maria Basto.

Manchuria

With all the goings-on at home, the missions still received first attention, and in the midst of building and having new expenses, and the growth in the Community, an invitation to work in another mission area was accepted. It was Manchuria, an area larger than Texas, to the north of Korea and northeast of China, This country, rich in mining and agriculture, had a population of 40 million. In 1840 there were only 2,000 Catholics. By 1923 they had grown to 30,000 in the southern vicariate alone.

The Maryknoll Society had been invited to come in 1926 and Fathers Raymond Lane and Joseph McCormack were assigned. Father Lane promptly put in his request for Maryknoll Sisters. The Maryknoll Society had two parishes in Dairen, Manchuria, a city of 200,000 Chinese and 70,000 Japanese.

The sisters arrived in 1930: Sisters Eunice Tolan, Gemma Shea, Angelica O'Leary and Coronata Sheehan from the States, and Sister Juliana Bedier from Hong Kong. The Maryknollers learned that Mother was arriving for a look-see. In spite of their most hopeful efforts to prepare the convent for Mother's arrival, they were hampered by the fact that their furniture was coming on the same boat with Mother. Sisters Columba Tarpey and Theodore Farley accompanied Mother, and there was a grand reunion.

In 1931 the sisters opened the Maryknoll Academy, an Elementary and High School in Dairen. Most of the pupils were Russians, whose families had left Russia upon the advent of Communism. Sisters Peter Duggan, Juliana Bedier, Famula, Coronata Sheehan and Ellen Mary Murphy were assigned. Two weeks after the opening of the Academy in Dairen, four sisters started a mission convent in the large open-cut coal-mining city of Fushun.

Manchuria was in a state of undeclared war when Sisters Eunice Tolan, Gloria Wagner, Veronica Marie Carney and de Lellis McKenna opened their convent in Fushun on October 9, 1931. The sisters' first two works were an orphanage with a school and a native novitiate.

The long-range wisdom of founding indigenous sisterhoods was apparent in the troubled years of war and Communist occupation to come. When all Maryknoll Sisters were repatriated from Manchuria and Korea during World War II, and expelled from South China in the early fifties, there were trained indigenous sisters ready to take over.

Our Lady of Maryknoll Statue

The statue of Our Lady of Maryknoll, a gift of Bishop Raymond A. Lane in 1936 in memory of Father Founder, and now in the Maryknoll Sisters Center foyer at Maryknoll, NY, was carved at the Fushun Mission by a non-Catholic, Lao Kuan. He allowed his children to be baptized during an illness, and as a result his wife decided to study the doctrine. She shortly became an enthusiastic Catholic, and won her husband to the Faith.

Some Other Events

~ **On snowy days in 1932** a team of farm horses pulled the sleigh carrying the sisters to their work in the Seminary kitchen and *The Field Afar* offices.

~ **In October 1932,** Mr. Potter, our first Physical Plant Engineer, with his wife and young daughter, moved into the house opposite the entrance to the Seminary at the corner of Brookside Lane, and it became known as *The Potter's House*. This was named *Refugium Peccatorum* (Refuge of Sinners), when some young Maryknoll Sisters lived their earlier!

A Reflective Moment

Throughout her life, Mother Mary Joseph
lovingly reached out to others,
not out of a need she had, but out of a fullness she possessed ~
the fruit of living consciously in the presence of God!

Resources

The above Reflections were adapted from:
To the Uttermost Parts of the Earth
by Camilla Kennedy, MM;
Maryknoll Sisters, A Pictorial History,
by Sister Mary Francis Louise, MM;
Maryknoll's First Lady by Jeanne Marie Lyons, MM;
On the Threshold of the Future
by Claudette LaVerdiere, MM;
1931-1935 Distaff (Sisters Diary) by Eunice Tolan, MM,
and Incarnata Farrelly, MM.

෨   ෨   ෨

#18 ~
The Contemplative Community

Standing: Sisters Marie Francois Combs, Rose Teresa McCullough, Christopher Naumann, MMJ, Magdalen Doelger, Dominica Gallagher, Rosalie Weber, Letitia Stephenson; *Sitting:* Sisters Rosaleen Hampson, Bernadette Mathieu and Irene Sullivan.

> At the 1997 General Assembly, the word "Cloister" was changed to "Contemplative Community," which expresses more clearly the life of prayer being lived rather than the structure.

Origin of Contemplative Community

In the mission spirituality of Mollie Rogers (Mother Mary Joseph), two words in particular can be highlighted as being of great importance to her: *Prayer and Mission*. Their roots within her were deeply touched, nourished and brought to a distinct fruition in 1914 when she accompanied Julia Ward on a trip to Rome. Visiting the Company of Mary, Blue Nuns, who had sisters praying continually before the Blessed Sacrament for their sisters, especially those who worked with nursing patients in their homes, Mother was touched deeply. It was then, she expressed:

There was born the idea of a contemplative branch for Maryknoll to complete our Maryknoll life, the vision of a group of sisters working solely by prayer for our absent ones and for the mission apostolate.

There is no doubting that the foundation of the Contemplative Community within Maryknoll was the innovative vision under God of Mother Mary Joseph alone. It was the culmination and completion of her mission ideal, *"Maryknoll Sisters praying unceasingly for all Maryknoll missioners and their works."* It was one of *"those delicate flowers of God which had been unfolding"* for a long time in Mother Mary Joseph's heart as it waited its moment in time to flower.

At the same time, Mother definitely held and firmly believed in *"the ideal and the idea that every Maryknoll Sister is a contemplative for every good missioner must be, accepting everything with our eyes fixed upon the face of Christ."*

In its early beginnings, the idea of prayer for missioners took the form of continuous periods of adoration before the Blessed Sacrament. Mother saw this early form enabling a development within the sisters of *"a sense of God's abiding presence"* which constituted the contemplative union with Christ in prayer essential to any real mission vocation.

Sister Magdalen Doelger (Marie Doelger)

In 1917 Sister Magdalen, who entered in 1916, made known to Sister Mary Joseph her desire for the contemplative way of life. Mother Mary Joseph recalled her promise at that time, saying: *"Well, have patience. Someday we are going to inaugurate a contemplative branch. I feel very strongly that we should have it to complete our Maryknoll life. This particular house will have prayer for the missions as its object."* As early as 1925, Mother was already contemplating a mission contemplative house and setting aside a sum for it, informing Sister Magdalen, *"I am keeping Sancian Island in mind for a House of Prayer ~ do not mention it ~ and I have a fund of $3,500 towards the convent, the gift of Sister Rosalie Weber's father. Sister Rosalie has the same desire as you have."*

Mother Mary Joseph's Personal Involvement in Establishing the Contemplative Community

Three years prior to the culmination of her dream of a contemplative branch, found Mother personally involved in every step toward her goal:

1) Visiting Archbishop McNicholas, OP, of Cincinnati with Sister Magdalen, as well as a Cloister Group there, following something along the lines Mother had in mind;

2) A personal interview in Rome with the Assistant Master General, Father Nolan, OP, who said: *It is the final stamp of the approval of God upon the work that the Maryknoll Sisters are doing.*

3) Assurance given to Sister Magdalen of a separate section of the Constitutions to safeguard the contemplative way of life; and

4) Mother Mary Joseph re-writing an adaptive version of the Second Order Dominican Rule.

Mother Mary Joseph, Father Walsh and Auxiliary Bishop John Dunn

Mother had explained to the Delegates at the 1931 Chapter that: *"Father General has always known of the plan and encouraged a very slow development. About three years ago, Father, who agreed with us that the time was approaching for the fulfillment of the idea, especially, perhaps, because Father James E. Walsh was longing for a contemplative group for his new China diocese, allowed us to present the matter to Auxiliary Bishop John Dunn (Archdiocese of NY). At first the Bishop was not inclined, thinking it could cause jealousy in the Community. I said I felt quite sure that the majority of sisters would welcome the idea. With the Bishop's approval, we organized and provided for such a development in connection with the preparation of our Constitutions."*

Assignments to Contemplative Community

The house designated for the Contemplative Community was the old Tompkins house cresting Maryknoll's highest hill. Mother said the Contemplative Community was *"simply another means we have taken of expressing our zeal for souls,"* calling it, *"the core of my heart."* While Mother was in the hospital, the formal announcement of the assignments was made on July 14, 1932.

Of the sisters who expressed a desire, ten sisters were chosen for this new venture: Sisters Marie (Magdalen) Doelger, Irene Sullivan, Bernadette (Ernestine) Mathieu, Christopher Naumann, Rose Teresa McCullough, Rosalie Weber, Dominica Gallagher, Letitia Stephenson, Rosaleen Hampson and Marie Francois Combs.

Mother's Continual Guidance

For Mother no detail was too insignificant in preparing for the blessed event. She was interested in every particular concerning the renovations at Regina Coeli; solicited funds herself for the enclosure fence; and from her hospital bed on July 14, 1932, inquired: *"Are you getting your utensils together? Is anybody giving you scales?* (Food was weighed out in Cloisters at that time.) *I suppose that will be quite as important as the food."* Upon returning to Maryknoll on August 7 after her hospital sojourn, Mother attended three days later the Breviary Classes conducted for the ten sisters by Father Tierney, OP. Later on, she offered the sisters the use of the Bishop Suite's veranda for an improvised choir and joined them whenever possible.

Delays in Starting the Contemplative Community

The group, eager to begin their long-cherished way of life, was to experience delays. Proposed dates were set up in that year 1932: Easter, Ascension Thursday, Pentecost, July 22, August 15. As each time approached, circumstances determined otherwise. The final trial came on August 12 with the news of an indefinite postponement pending Cardinal Hayes' approval. And he was ill!

Mother's Retreat to the Contemplative Community

Still in the dark as to the Cardinal's approval for the establishment of the House of Prayer, Mother held out promise of a retreat toward the end of September. It actually began on September 24, and the retreat embraced Mother's spiritual treasury to them of the significance of their lives as missionary contemplatives within the larger Maryknoll Sisters Congregation.

First and always they were to be Maryknoll Sisters: *"Your house is simply another Maryknoll house. The Cloister (Contemplative Community) will be an integral part of Maryknoll with a different kind of work to do."* She envisioned them set apart to dedicate their lives to a *"work of prayer and loving contemplation, a work of penance and of sacrifice with some manual labor to keep minds sane and bodies healthy,"* all for the sake of the mission apostolate. She spoke, also, on the particular difficulties that were a struggle for all missioners, like loneliness. She wanted the sisters to root their contemplative life in an ever-deepened knowledge and love of the missions.

Permission for Contemplative Community

God's loving Providence shone forth so clearly in all that transpired on the very last day of the sisters' retreat together. As the group assembled in Mother's room for their final conference on the Feast of St. Therese, October 3, 1932, her talk on Eternal Life became a prelude to the great announcement that Auxiliary Bishop Dunn had telephoned the previous day giving the gladsome news of Cardinal Hayes' permission for the Contemplative Community's foundation. Bishop John Dunn himself would preside the following day at the Enclosure Ceremony, October 4.

Enclosure Ceremony

The Enclosure Ceremony at Regina Coeli and the Dedication of the Altar in the Motherhouse Chapel by Auxiliary Bishop Dunn, celebrated that same October 4, made the day a very full one for all. The marble Altar was a gift to the Congregation from Bishop Dunn.

That evening after all the busyness had subsided, Mother wended her way up to the hilltop for a first visit with her daughters, bringing for each the cherished little souvenir of a Dominican Missal lovingly inscribed, and when goodbyes were said, leaving behind ten hearts that beat high with hope in the joy of their missionary contemplative vocation.

Contemplative Community Dedication and Final Enclosure

From those early days onward, it was Mother Mary Joseph who gave the sisters on the hilltop their particular dedication: Sister Magdalen of Jesus, Sister Christopher of the Child Jesus and the Holy Face, Sister Rosalie of the Holy Family, Sister Irene of the Holy Spirit, etc. Mother, herself, chose the title, *of the Annunciation,* and ordinarily spent March 25 at *Regina Coeli* celebrating her feastday in a special way.

On the Final Enclosure Day on October 3, 1934, Mother announced: *"It has seemed wise to us to have these sisters spend the day before Final Enclosure at the Motherhouse, living again the common life of the Congregation, observing no fast, nor saying the Divine Office. They will come for meditation and remain for evening Benediction ~ the inauguration of a beautiful custom signifying the deep relationship between the Contemplative Group and the Congregation."*

Mother Mary Joseph's Continued Solicitude

Mother's solicitude even over the smallest things is lovingly manifested in a little note to Sister Magdalen on March 1, 1934, expressing her concern and saying: *"I thought of you during the storm and wondered if you had milk. I knew you had canned things and would not starve, but I was anxious about the milk and eggs."* Mother graced the approach of the Fifth Anniversary of Enclosure through a series of conferences, confidently expressing in the very first paragraph her role as the *"Planter and Tenderer of the Garden Enclosed."*

Mother's Gentle Guidance

An outstanding example of Mother's gentle guidance shines through in the following incident. Sister Magdalen's heart was set on using the Second Order Dominican Rule and making solemn vows, basically to safeguard the cloistered life. Knowing that their becoming a formal Second Order would mean the impossibility of remaining attached to Maryknoll, Mother revealed her magnanimous soul in a letter to Sister Magdalen on June 13, 1930, while she was away on visitation.

....Basing my thoughts on the letter I had received (Sister Magdalen's letter of February 18, 1930) I said I was forcing myself to realize that I should not ask the impossible of your little group ~ and I would have to let you make your decision on my return.

In 1936 the sisters in the Contemplative Community requested that their first *Particular Rule* be dropped and that they be governed by the *Maryknoll Sisters Constitutions* with its Cloister Section; and, like the rest of the Congregation, simply have a Directory. This pleased Mother very much. She commented on this fact to the Chapter Delegates on July 16, 1937, acknowledging with satisfaction:

It seems to me that this takes away the last slightest shadow between them and us. They are part of us as much as we belong to them. We have our Directory governing our works, and they are to have a Directory governing theirs. Under it they are just as much subject to us, as are any of you.

Mother had a number of sessions with the sisters on the Directory, was consulted all along the way and approved the final draft.

Mother's Visits to the Hilltop

Mother really enjoyed her days within the enclosure, a list of special ones becoming traditional: her Cloister Feast of the Annunciation, Sister Magdalen's Feastday on July 22; September 8, Birthday Party in honor of Our Lady; October 3, St. Therese's Feast and the Foundation Day of the Contemplative Community; December 28, the Holy Innocents Party. These were not the only times she delighted the sisters with her presence in their midst. Right up to her being stricken by paralysis on March 23, 1952, Mother's role of inspiration and guidance was lovingly and appreciatively received by her community on the hilltop.

Mother assisted them at that particular time with the Supplement to the Directory. The Hilltop Diary for the fateful day of her serious illness reads in sorrowing tones:

Before Terce, Sister Mary Theodore assembled the community to announce a pleasant surprise planned for tomorrow, the anticipation of which might be enjoyed throughout Laetare Sunday. Mother Mary Joseph of the Annunciation would be with us for Solemn Chapter on the Vigil of the Annunciation and afterwards remain to devote a day's work to our Supplement of the Directory; then Mother would stay overnight in Maison Therese and officiate at Midnight Office of her own Cloister Feastday. What a happy surprise this announcement was!

The few necessary preparations had been made: Mother's chair brought down from the attic, and everything seemed ready for St. Gabriel's Day, when suddenly in mid-afternoon our hopes were changed into anxious fears. Mother Mary Columba telephoned that Mother Mary Joseph had been stricken with paralysis and was in a critical condition. With heavy hearts we spent the rest of Laetare Sunday in vigils before the Blessed Sacrament for our beloved Mother.

Mother's Last Visit

On October 3, 1955, a few days before her death, Mother was driven up the hill in her wheelchair, accompanied by two nurses, to spend a good part of St. Therese's Feastday, keeping the tradition that went back to the Contemplative Community's foundation. She brought white roses, the latest Garden Encyclopedia, and a box of sweets. She looked less well than the last time she had visited, but she entered with much animation into the joy of the celebration. Around three o'clock, Mother Mary Columba drove up to call for her in order to give her some rest before Lily Windsor's concert in the evening. The following Saturday, before Mass began, we were startled to learn of her departure by ambulance for St. Vincent's Hospital and having surgery at noon.

All through Saturday night, and on Sunday hour by hour, the Contemplative Community, united with the entire Congregation, kept vigil in spirit beside her bed. On that Sunday, October 9, while the Contemplative Community was singing the *Magnificat* at Vespers, Mother Mary Joseph gave back her precious soul to God.

A Reflective Moment

Mother Mary Joseph is in our hearts, and we know that where there is love, distance is crossed by the bridge of love. Together with her prayerful spirit, we are daily grateful for the gift of our missionary/contemplative vocation that is given to all members!

Resources

The above Reflections were adapted from:
To the Uttermost Parts of the Earth by Camilla Kennedy, MM;
Mother Mary Joseph's Conference, October 1934;
Into the Heart of Mission, Booklet on the Contemplative Community
by Madeline McHugh, MM;
Maryknoll's First Lady by Jeanne Marie Lyons, MM;
On the Threshold of the Future by Claudette LaVerdiere, MM.

಄   ಄   ಄

#19 ~ Bishop James Anthony Walsh

Consecration of Bishop Walsh
in Rome - 1933

For Mother Mary Joseph one of the greatest joys of these years was Father Walsh's consecration as Titular Bishop of Siene on June 29, 1933, the 22nd anniversary of the Maryknoll Society's Foundation. By then, there were over 900 Maryknollers to rejoice in the honor that the Church had bestowed on the Maryknoll Founder. He had, since the earliest days of his priesthood, an antipathy for honors without responsibility; but on being offered the fullness of the priesthood, he accepted it with honest happiness. He saw in the action of the Holy Father, Pope Pius XI, not only a commendation of Maryknoll and its work, but an appreciation of the role which the Catholics of his country were beginning to play in the mission of the Church. Mother Mary Joseph and Sister Mary Xavier O'Donnell joined a group of Walsh's friends ~ priests, bishops and laity ~ who accompanied him on the ship to Europe for the ceremony in Rome.

Day of the Ceremony

The day of the ceremony, the Feast of Sts. Peter and Paul, June 29, 1933, dawned with clouds and showers, but the sky cleared and the sun came to throw its golden cloak over the beautiful city of Rome. Mother Mary Joseph knew one of those rare moments when the world seems a very heaven. Mother's heart was full as she watched Father Walsh move forward in the colorful line of dignitaries, companioned by those who valued and appreciated him, the consecrator, Cardinal Pietro Fumasoni-Biondi, and the co-consecrators, Auxiliary Bishop John J. Dunn of the New York Archdiocese, and Archbishop John T. McNicholas, OP, of Cincinnati, Ohio. Suddenly she, who in a lifetime conceded few tears either to pain or grief, saw Father Walsh's energetic figure, his grave and alert face, through a haze of tears. Few, if any, knew so well the long traveling through the dark ways of faith which had brought him to this auspicious moment.

When following the singing of the *Veni Sancte Spiritus,* which he loved so much, he made his prostration and lay clear-minded and petitioning before the altar of God. Mother knew herself to be at one with all that he asked of God.

Illness of Bishop James A. Walsh

Bishop James Anthony Walsh, who was sixty-six years old when he became bishop, appeared to be healthy. Within the year, however, he needed to take time off for treatments, which everyone believed would restore his health. He spent the early months of 1935 in the warm climate of Jacksonville, Florida, at St. Vincent's Hospital. In a letter from Florida, dated March 18, 1935, and addressed to *Dear Mother M. J.,* he indicated much leisure to think in the past few months, and that our sisters have often been the subject of his thoughts. Remembering that Maryknoll was twenty-five years from its beginnings, he indicated what was in his thoughts:

> *Before you and I pass on, we should try to formulate definite policies of mutual relations for the two societies, as well as methods of co-operation. I have encouraged independence of your society, since canonically, mine has no right to control its affairs. I believe, however, that we should act as big interested brothers whose counsel and protection you would do well to seek....that you should make more frequent approaches not only personally but especially with your council.*

The Bishop returned to Maryknoll in April and resumed his role as Father General. Although he was not well enough to participate in the administration of the Society, in June he ordained sixteen priests and presided at the departure ceremony on July 30, 1933, giving again his customary words of encouragement to fourteen priests and one brother about to leave for their first mission assignments in South China, Korea, Manchuria and Manila, and the first group assigned to Japan. He preferred not to be called *Bishop,* but rather *Father* or *Father General,* especially within the Maryknoll family.

Consecration of Monsignor Francis X. Ford in the Maryknoll Sisters' Chapel

In April 1935, news had arrived from South China that Monsignor Francis X. Ford, Vicar Apostolic of Kaying Prefecture, had been named Bishop. Father Ford had been the first student to arrive at Maryknoll in September 1912 and was in the first group of Maryknoll Missioners to go to China in 1918. He specifically requested that his ordination be at Maryknoll and by his own Father General, Bishop James Anthony Walsh.

Bishop Walsh remained surprisingly well as he anticipated this privilege. Monsignor Ford's ordination to the episcopacy on September 21, 1935, seemed to be a culmination and fulfillment of Bishop Walsh's life. It was also a magnificent moment for Mother Mary Joseph, as Bishop Ford looked to her as a spiritual mother. The consecration was held in the Motherhouse Chapel of the Annunciation. The experience of the event was caught in the words of Mother's letter addressed to all Maryknollers around the world:

The heart of every Maryknoller was thrilled and overflowing with gratitude that Bishop Walsh was there, so austere, yet so benign - and somehow - so fragile.

Serious Illness of Bishop James A. Walsh

By mid-October, 1935, Bishop Walsh's health had deteriorated noticeably. Mother Mary Joseph received a poignant note from him on her fifty-third birthday, October 27, thanking her for her "*devoted, loyal, friendship: You have been to me a sister and my prayer in gratitude for the privilege is that God may give you abundant graces for the years of service that lie ahead for you.*" As always, the Maryknoll Sister-nurses attended him and Mother kept a watchful eye filled with careful love during the last days and hours of his earthly life.

It was clear now that Bishop Walsh was dying of lung cancer. In December 1935, he was conscious that he had not seen all of his Maryknoll family for a long time. Since the sisters were not as accessible as the priests, seminarians and brothers, he thought it would be good to see them soon. Before breakfast on December 22, Mother shared with the sisters in the refectory: "*Father General has asked to see all the professed sisters. This morning at ten o'clock the bell will ring for you to go over to the Seminary together. When you reach Father's room, go in one by one. Kneel and kiss his ring. Do not delay. Do not talk, and do not cry. Father does not have the same control over his emotions that he has always had. It is going to be an ordeal, physically, for him, but he wants to see you.*" Mother went often to see Bishop Walsh, to attend Mass when it was said in his room, to do some service, to see that the sister-nurses had everything that they needed for his comfort, simply to companion him briefly or to pray with and for him.

Death of Bishop James A. Walsh

On Easter Monday, 1936, Dr. Sweet, who had grown to love Bishop Walsh, found that his right lung was completely filled up. It was evident that the end was not far away. On Tuesday morning, April 14, around eight o'clock, Father Drought called Mother Mary Joseph to come.

When she saw Father Walsh, Mother knew that the *consummatum est* would be soon. Mother later shared:

> *Sisters Lillian and Agnes Regina, the nurses, Father Drought and myself were with him. The priests came in, gave him their blessings and passed into the private chapel just beyond his room and recited the prayers for the dying. He was conscious to the end, missing none of the prayers for the dying or the rosary led by Father Drought. Very shortly before the last breath came, I repeated the ejaculation, 'Jesus, Mary, Joseph' and he answered audibly, 'I give you my heart and my soul.'*

For Mother Mary Joseph the death of Bishop Walsh was a deeply spiritual experience of pain and wonder, of aloneness and appreciation, of sorrow and joy, of loss and hope. The last of the three Maryknoll Founders, she would live on for nearly twenty years, faithfully bearing witness to the spirit and charism of Maryknoll.

Funeral Services

In the days that followed, Masses were offered and watches kept by the Founder's body, first at the Seminary, then at the Motherhouse, and finally at St. Patrick's Cathedral in New York. This great Church was solidly packed for the final Mass offered by Archbishop Mooney and presided over by Cardinal Hayes. Archbishop McNicholas compressed into his sermon much of the affection and admiration which he had had for his dear friend over the years. Immediately after the Funeral Mass, Mother set to work on an article which the Maryknoll Fathers had asked her to write for the May issue of *The Field Afar,* planned as a memorial issue for their Father Founder.

Bishop Walsh's Farewell Message

Bishop Walsh had prepared a moving farewell message for each branch of the Maryknoll family. In part, these were his last formal words to the sisters:

> *Before leaving earth, let me acknowledge that I owe to your community no small portion of the success which has been credited to Maryknoll. Your generous and capable services and, above all, your constant prayers, have been with Maryknoll from the beginning. No one knows this better than I, and no one should be more grateful....I leave with you the affection of a father for his daughters, my one regret being that in these later years I could not know you individually as I would. It is a comforting thought that Mother Mary Joseph is being spared for your guidance and inspiration. May God keep her strong for many years to come.*

Excerpts from Mother Mary Joseph's Reflections in The Field Afar - May 1936

I speak for the daughters of the Maryknoll household. I speak as one who knows, out of years of blessed friendship and privileged association with our Father General. With the Church at large we recognize and admire the achievements of his fine mind, the accomplishments of which made him a world figure. Of these much will be said by others, while we look happily back and ponder on the little things of yesterday that made him for us the beloved head of a growing family.

From the very beginning there were the substantial elements of this triple-branched family - the students, Maryknoll's future missioners; lay helpers, the future auxiliary brotherhood; and the secretaries, Maryknoll's Sisters-to-be. We were closely bound by a common interest, the missions, by a strong spirit of mutual helpfulness, and by a common Father's affectionate protection. The early days at Maryknoll were idyllic, our lives pastoral. Father Walsh seldom had two coins to jingle in his pocket; the houses, though only an hour from Broadway, were devoid of the most ordinary conveniences, and we literally lived from one day to another. But we were profoundly happy and at peace.

The woman's part was quite naturally ours. While the seminarians made their studies or worked with the brothers in house and field, we found joy in serving them as cook, laundress, seamstress and secretary....Then there was our live-stock, almost a part of the family, sheep and oxen, horses and mules, pigs, chickens and cows. When a new calf or lambs came, we were notified and Father would accompany us to greet and name the little strangers: Prima, Secunda, Hibernia, Patricia, Thomasina and Aquinas were all our pets. The students and brothers did much planting and in direct ratio there was preserving and canning. Often as we prepared vegetables and fruits in the evening, Father would visit us and in his inimitable way tell us of his experiences at home and abroad, till weary bodies and aching feet were forgotten. Or he would drop in on his way from the city to leave with his "Marys" a box of sweets.

Whenever possible, he visited our homes and brought us direct news from our loved ones....Our days were filled with hard, even laborious, work and simple pleasures shared by all - and no one envied us! Nor had the more important side of our life been for a moment neglected. There was a horarium from the first day and there were guidelines, simple suggestions for religious conduct and right thinking.

Here are a few of Father Walsh's Guidelines:

➢ *Cultivate tact*
   a) Try to get at the other's viewpoint.
   b) Find and admit what is good in any proposition before objecting.

➢ *Recall high ideals of sacrifice expected of missionaries.*

➢ *Flee jealousy as a serpent.*

➢ *Politeness is not enough among Christians. It should be only the outward expression of tender solicitude and love in and for Christ.*

➢ *A place for everything and everything in its place.*

➢ *Make a difference between feast and fast day fare.*

A quarter of a century has rolled on since our beginning....the same high ideals have been kept before us, the same lofty counsels presented to us and the same unbroken spirit of cooperation throughout the Maryknoll Family expected of us....Some of us were privileged to be with Father through his last illness, which revealed his lifelong character – strength and tenderness, patience and forbearance, considerateness of others, lofty courage, an indomitable will under the refining influence of a noble humility, unshaken confidence in God's plan for him.

Bishop James A. Walsh was buried in a temporary grave in the Maryknoll Society's Cemetery. The body of Father Thomas F. Price had been buried at Maryknoll, NY, on December 8, 1936. In 1955, their remains were transferred to the crypt under the newly completed Seminary Chapel.

A Reflective Moment
Bishop Walsh's death was a sacred moment
for Mother Mary Joseph and the Maryknoll Family.
His journey, Father Price's and Mother's are essential to the Dream
that is MARYKNOLL, as is our own, today and into the future!

Resources
The above Reflections were adapted from:
To the Uttermost Parts of the Earth by Camilla Kennedy, MM;
Maryknoll's First Lady by Jeanne Marie Lyons, MM;
On the Threshold of the Future by Claudette LaVerdiere, MM;
As One Lamp Lights Another by Barbara Hendricks, MM;
1936 Distaff by Eunice Tolan, MM, and Incarnata Farrelly, MM;
and 1936 May issue of *The Field Afar.*

ଽୠ   ଽୠ   ଽୠ

Sister Madeleine Sophie Karlon's direct evangelization in China in the 1930's.

Direct Evangelization

When the first group of sisters disembarked at Yeungkong in 1922, Father Francis Ford welcomed them graciously. A year later on the occasion of Mother Mary Joseph's first visit to China, he described the special attraction of the sisters for women and children and alluded for the first time to the important role religious women could fill in apostolic work. When Father Ford shared his views with Mother, he discovered that she, too, envisioned a life of apostolic work for her sisters. Her approval opened the way for the Maryknoll Sisters' direct apostolate in China.

A New Venture

In March 1924, Father Ford took Sisters Rose Leifels and Lawrence Foley on an extended mission trip for a whole week. In each outstation, while the Fathers administered the sacraments and met with the men, the sisters spent their time with the women. This included: visiting in their homes, mingling with them while the catechist, Rosa, gave daily instructions, and staying for chats before and after the evening prayers. In their report, the two sisters described themselves as two *"happy missioners who experienced a week of sleeping on Chinese beds, eating Chinese food, and speaking the Chinese language."* The excitement of Sisters Rose and Lawrence was soon shared by the other sisters in Yeungkong.

Anti-Foreign Incidents

The recall of the sisters to the safety of Hong Kong following the anti-foreign incidents of June 1925 in Canton and the assignment of Father Ford to Kaying in the fall of the same year put an end to the experiment, and Father Ford had to postpone his plan for nine years. Finally in 1934, he invited the Maryknoll Sisters to Hakkaland for the exclusive purpose of evangelizing the women, leading them to embrace Catholicism, instructing them for baptism, and watching over them during their first years as new Catholics.

His request received the full approval of the Maryknoll Sisters' leadership in China, Sister Mary Paul McKenna, and Mother Mary Joseph gave Father Ford all the sisters he requested. In 1935, fourteen sisters were assigned to China, four being sent to Kaying. In 1936, Mother wrote to Father Ford, "*The sisters are most enthusiastic over their work in Kaying and the ones at home are all clamoring to be assigned to what seems to be the ideal life for one who is called to missionary work.*"

Election of Bishop James Edward Walsh
The death of Bishop James A. Walsh affected profoundly the whole Maryknoll Family. At their General Chapter held in Hong Kong in 1936, the priests and brothers of the Maryknoll Society elected on September 7, 1936, Bishop James Edward Walsh as the second Superior General. He had been one of the first Maryknollers to arrive in China in 1918, and in 1927 had been made Bishop of the Kongmoon Vicariate. The ceremony was on Sancian Island. Mother penned the news to her *dear ones everywhere.* In the Maryknoll Family, Mother fostered a unity which, at the same time, enhanced the integrity of each entity. Bishop James E. Walsh was also the first to write back to Maryknoll in 1920 regarding mission openings for the sisters, even before they were officially recognized as a religious congregation.

Monsignor William E. Cashin
From 1912 to Father Walsh's death in 1936, he was the Maryknoll Sisters Ecclesiastical Superior. Monsignor William E. Cashin, a very dear friend of Mother Mary Joseph and uncle of Sisters Helen and William Eugene Cashin, was then appointed by Cardinal Hayes to this position.

Maryknoll Kindergarten
In late 1936, a kindergarten was opened in the Motherhouse at Maryknoll, NY, with the hope that it would be a paying proposition, and be good for the Normal School students. Sister Clare Marie Tivnan was teacher and chauffeur for eight youngsters whom she taught in St. Philomena's Hall (Infirmary Annex). The mission field for the sisters had widened to Kaying on October 18, 1933, Shanghai on March 12, 1935 and Japan on June 5, 1937.

Opening *of 1937 General Chapter*
The Chapter meetings took place every six years at the Maryknoll Sisters Center in NY, and became increasingly important as a context of clarification and decision-making for the entire community. By the end of the 1930's, the United States, along with the rest of the world, was on the verge of the Second World War.

On July 7, 1937, a Japanese Military contingent on maneuvers clashed with a unit of Chinese soldiers south of Peiping. Only one week later, on July 13, 1937, Maryknoll Sister delegates from their missions in China, Korea, Manchuria, the Philippines, Hawaii and the United States gathered at Maryknoll, New York, for their third General Chapter. All delegates had arrived by late June. The Philippine delegation brought their postulant, Irmgard Baumann (Sr. Marie Elise) of German descent. A full-length picture of her in shorts, as *Far East Tennis Champion*, appeared on the first page of a Philippine newspaper and was posted on the ship's bulletin board!

Little did the sisters realize when they came together in 1937 that World War II would make it impossible to have another Chapter meeting until 1946.

Delegates to the 1937 Chapter
The Delegates were: Mother Mary Joseph, Sisters M. Trinita Logue, M. Felicita Clarke, M. Columba Tarpey, M. de Paul Cogan, M. Mark Killoran, M. Martina Bridgeman, M. Colman Coleman, M. Paul McKenna, M. Theodore Farley, M. Eunice Tolan, M. Sylvester Collins, Marie Therese Kehoe, M. Ephrem Griffin, Virginia Marie Lynn, M. Judith Tivnan, M. Veronica Hartman, M. Juliana Bedier, M. Amadeus McCallister, M. Patricia Coughlin, M. Redempta Coffey, Regina Reardon, M. Regis McKenna and M. Esther Coveny.

Opening Session of the Third Chapter
The Chapter began on July 10 after the Mass of the Holy Spirit with meetings held in one of the Normal School classrooms. A significant event was the opening talk by Bishop James E. Walsh, who had years of mission experience with the Maryknoll Sisters in China. He highlighted clearly, for the very first time, the role of the sisters as *actual missioners* rather than *helpers of missionaries*. That clarification caused Mother to put into words what all the sisters felt: "*Never has anyone spoken to us in this way before.*" Mother recalled that each sister in those early days held in her heart as deep a yearning to go to the missions as the sisters do today, but it seemed hopeless then. It was not even the idea of Father James A Walsh in the early days.

The aim of the sisters to do mission work had always been clear and they had worked ceaselessly to attain it, but in Mother's words, "*We have never been able to get from the Society a statement as Bishop James E. Walsh made this morning. He made it plain to the sisters what is our position and place in the apostolate.*"

The Bishop began his talk by giving a stirring commendation of the contribution of the Maryknoll Sisters in China from 1921 through 1937. He then continued: *"Your vocation consists in being missioners the same as the priests....You do everything and anything connected with mission work, and you should consider yourselves apostles. You are a missionary congregation, and the emphasis with you would be in evangelical work, the same as in our own case. You are not merely a group of auxiliaries....doing what you are told. You brought something new ~ the woman's apostolate."* Bishop James E. Walsh's understanding of the role of women in mission was remarkable for that era.

Election of Officers

Later in the day, the Community heard the names of the newly-elected Officers: Mother Mary Joseph Rogers as Mother General, Sister Mary Columba Tarpey as Vicaress General, Sister Mary Eunice Tolan as 2nd Councilor and Secretary General, Sister Marie Therese Kehoe as 3rd Councilor and SisterMary Annette Kelley as 4th Councilor and Treasurer General.

Mother's election for a third term as Mother General needed to go as a *postulation* to Rome via Cardinal Hayes. Sister Columba, as Secretary of the Chapter, sent this to Cardinal Hayes, together with a request that Mother Mary Joseph be confirmed as Mother General for life. (Mother Samuel of Sinsinawa and Mother Kathryn Drexel of the Blessed Sacrament Sisters had received this permission.)

On July 14, Cardinal Hayes confirmed Mother for a third term. He said he was going away and would take up the matter *for life* in September. When the Cardinal returned to his residence in September, he did not respond to the request. Sister Mary Columba wrote him again, but he never replied. We later learned he was ill. He died September 4, 1938.

Chapter Session at the Cloister

The Contemplative Community had been developing for five years in the mission ideals set forth by Mother Mary Joseph. For the first time an official session of the Chapter was held at *Regina Coeli*. Mother and the Delegates walked the stone's throw distance up to Maryknoll's hilltop. Mother, who presided at this session, articulated her understanding of the unique but natural position of the Contemplative Community in the life of the Maryknoll Sisters:

I never go back on the ideal and the idea that every Maryknoll Sister is a contemplative. And when I say 'contemplative,' I do not mean in the sense of one set apart to dwell upon the things of God. I mean that we must be so trained, formed in our affections, our inward gaze fixed solely upon God, and no matter what distractions, no matter what works, what trials ~ always our first thought is to face everything with our eyes fixed upon the face of Christ. I think it is the cause of the joy that dominates the life of every Maryknoll Sister ~ union with God.

Closing Session, July 31, 1937

After a short two weeks, this third Chapter drew to a close. Mother Mary Joseph reflected what the sisters experienced, *"I think you realize as I do, almost perhaps for the first time, that we are, as a congregation, maturing, growing mellow, increasing in love for one another in the highest interpretation of that word."* Mother was aware of a breadth of vision. Each and all the sisters were able to distinguish between what constituted a real good for the whole community from what seemed desirable only for individuals within the community. She said: *"I have never before been so assured of our solidity as during these days."*

War Escalating

The General Assembly of 1937 terminated within two weeks. By August, renewed and affirmed, the delegates would be traveling back to their various missions. Most sisters did not realize that a full-scale war had begun. By November 1937, all along the coast of South China from north to south, the signs of warfare appeared in the skies, the rivers and the countryside. With war planes, gunboats, transports and troops, the Japanese Empire steadily bombed and assumed control of many populated areas, as well as travel and communication systems.

Rome's Blessing on the Sisters' Direct Evangelization

The future of the Kaying method of direct evangelization by the sisters remained uncertain, because it was only an experiment that the Holy See could discontinue at any time. The sisters pioneered a new approach by going out to the people, often living for weeks at a time in the homes of the villagers. That sisters should live away from their convents without daily Mass, caused considerable criticism by some religious orders in China.

Finally, in March 1939, Cardinal Pietro Fumasoni-Biondi, the Prefect of the Sacred Congregation for the Propagation of the Faith, wrote a letter to Mother Mary Joseph, telling her of Rome's approval and blessings on the sisters' direct evangelization ministry, praising the contribution made by the sisters in going out in twos to the Hakka villages. Such work and sacrifice, the Cardinal indicated, *"showed courage and devotion."*

A Reflective Moment
As those who have gone before us,
we live hopefully and prophetically in mission,
giving ourselves away in love!

Resources
The above Reflections were adapted from:
To the Uttermost Parts of the Earth by Camilla Kennedy, MM;
Maryknoll in China by Jean-Paul Wiest;
On the Threshold of the Future by Claudette LaVerdiere, MM;
As One Lamp Lights Another by Barbara Hendricks, MM;
1932-1941 Distaff (Sisters Diary)
by Eunice Tolan, MM, and Incarnata Farrelly, MM.

൭   ൭   ൭

1940 ~ Mother Mary Joseph leaving for the Orient.

1937 ~ Mother Mary Joseph's Visit to the Sisters in Asia Delayed

Events both in Europe and in the Far East became increasingly ominous during the late thirties when news from our mission areas caused much dismay. Mother Mary Joseph was yearning to visit the sisters in Asia to know firsthand what they were facing. She had intended to start out immediately after the 1937 General Chapter, but the unwillingness of the State Department to issue a passport for travel in China caused her to wait in hopes of better conditions, and then her own illnesses delayed her. Mother suffered a long series of illnesses which began in the fall of 1938 and dragged on through 1939. These illnesses were diagnosed as a heart attack, very high temperatures, flu and finally in May 1939, a hernia. During these long months the diaries recorded that she was *"on a reduced schedule."*

Mother's Trip to the Orient in 1940

It was late spring of 1940 that Mother experienced renewed vigor and decided to set out to visit the sisters on the West Coast, Hawaii and, hopefully, Asia. After visiting the various Maryknoll schools, social services and catechetical programs in Hawaii, she sailed for Asia, reaching Japan after having lived through the fright of a hundred and twenty mile an hour hurricane. The ship made two brief stops in Japan. The vessel eventually limped into Shanghai where Sister M. Paul McKenna was awaiting Mother.

"The poverty on all sides was appalling," Mother wrote her sisters at home, *"soldiers ~ British, French, Japanese and U.S. Marines ~ were everywhere, and there was over all a tenseness that made living in the troubled sections very trying on the nerves."* Nor was the news from Europe good. Hitler's forces had streamlined across Europe and taken Belgium and France.

Hong Kong

When Mother reached Hong Kong on her birthday, October 27, 1940, she found the British Colony readying for war with blackouts and mock battles. Worried about her sisters on the mainland, she realized it was impossible to cross Japanese lines. Moreover, there were no boats to take her and she was already suffering from malaria. Three nights after her arrival, Mother stayed up on the convent roof with the sisters until late, watching a simulated attack on Hong Kong. At another time, she undertook to take movies of the waiting crowds at one of the soup kitchens where her sisters were working. The 1,700 people on the line thronged around her so that she could hardly move, much less focus a camera. She visited the two large schools the sisters had established. Living in the shadow of the Sino-Japanese war, the sisters hoped their efforts and all the other projects they had initiated to meet the needs of the colony: soup kitchens, clinics, food and clothing distribution, training of emergency volunteers, teaching catechism, visiting hospitals ~ would not grind to a halt.

Philippines

In mid-November 1940, Mother Mary Joseph set out for her visitation of the sisters in the Philippines, which was the fifth country of overseas mission for the Maryknoll Sisters Congregation. The Malabon Normal School had opened in June 1926. In the early thirties the Archdiocese was no longer able to support the project financially. It was Mother's vision of the school's importance which saved the situation. She agreed to support the sisters and in 1934 Mother and her Council would take on total responsibility for the Normal School.

Mother Mary Joseph soon set out on her visit to each of the missions in the Philippines, all of which were located on the large northern Island of Luzon. She observed and listened to all that had been accomplished since the sisters' arrival in January 1926 and, in particular, during the ten years since her last visit in 1930. In the midst of widespread rumors of all-out war, she counseled the sisters to keep their hearts focused on God's faithfulness regardless of the odds. Mother Mary Joseph left the Philippines with high hopes for the future.

She realized that mission in the Philippines had brought many blessings to the Maryknoll Sisters, one of which was the call to mission of five young Filipina women during the prewar period. However, in December 1941, the Japanese army would invade and take control of Manila, terminating all the missions and the outreach activity of the Maryknoll Sisters.

End of the Visitation

Although Mother Mary Joseph had hoped to visit the sisters in all the missions, the encroaching war made this impossible. She cabled the northern missions of China, Manchuria and Korea from Manila, and the sisters who were able to do so traveled to the port cities in those countries for a brief visit aboard ship, just as the sisters from Japan and Shanghai had done. Mother wended her way back to Maryknoll, NY, on December 28, 1940. No matter how brief these visits were, the memory of Mother Mary Joseph's loving and serene presence sustained the sisters all through the war years.

Sisters' Decision to Remain in War Area

As war news from Asia and Europe seeped through the media, Mother faced a very difficult decision. In the time of war should the Maryknoll Sisters remain in their Asian missions? The tradition of the Catholic Church was that missioners remained with the people to whom they had been sent, regardless of cost or pain. Maryknollers took this for granted. The United States government, however, was advising its nationals to leave Asia in order to avoid internment as enemy aliens. Trusting in God's providence, and after consultation with local church authorities, Mother and her Council decided the sisters would stay in their missions.

Pearl Harbor

On December 7, 1941, at 7:40 a.m., the first Japanese bombers reached the Hawaiian Islands where the tragic attack on Pearl Harbor took place. A few hours later the Japanese Military attacked the Philippines where on the Island of Luzon there were 53 Maryknoll Sisters. They likewise bombed Guam and landed troops in the Malay Peninsula. Meanwhile, Japanese police and soldiers arrived at the gates and doors of all Maryknoll missions throughout Korea and Manchuria. They came to intern or imprison American nationals, Priests, Brothers and Sisters and, as time permitted, to interrogate. On December 11, Congress declared war on Japan; three days later Germany, in support of their ally, declared war against the States.

Fall of Hong Kong

On December 12, 1941, following five days of attack, Kowloon, the mainland city of the Crown Colony of Hong Kong, fell to the Japanese Army. On Christmas Day, Hong Kong, too, had fallen. During this initial period, the missioners were treated simply as interned aliens. In April and in June 1942, some Maryknoll Sisters were released from internment at Stanley prison, ten of them to go aboard the exchange ship, *Asama Maru,* for the first lap of their return to the States; the rest to make their way in small groups for Kwang Cho Waan via Macao.

Asama Maru Exchange Ship

Aboard the exchange ship, *Asama Maru,* the sisters from Hong Kong found among the passengers twenty-one other Maryknoll Sisters from Korea and Manchuria, as well as a number of Maryknoll Priests and Brothers. In Portuguese East Africa, the ship's hundreds of passengers would be exchanged with the Japanese nationals arriving from the West on the *S.S. Gripsholm.* The *Gripsholm* completed its voyage and sailed up the Hudson River on August 25, 1942. The sisters on board found Mother waiting at the pier to welcome them ~ with deep joy in her heart to have them home safely. During the slow processing of passengers by the Federal Bureau of Investigation, she stayed the entire three days, returning in triumph with the last two sisters to be released. They drove up at night to a Motherhouse ablaze with lights, and with grateful, loving sisters coming out of its doors and down its steps to welcome the returnees and accompany them inside to the Chapel for a *Te Deum.*

S.S. Gripsholm's Second Voyage

After the first return of her sisters as exchange prisoners on the *S.S. Gripsholm* in August of 1942, Mother Mary Joseph received little detailed information about her sisters in war-torn Asia until the following year. In December of 1943, the *Gripsholm* again arrived in Jersey City with thirty-two Maryknollers from Manchuria and Japan: nineteen sisters, twelve priests, and one brother. Mother did her best to follow the distant war, but the ordinary channels of communication with her sisters were blocked for the remainder of the war years.

Los Baños

In May 1942, 12,500 Americans and over 60,000 Filipinos surrendered unconditionally. Since January of that year, except for a few Maryknoll Sisters not restricted either for reasons of nationality or of health, all the others had been interned by Japanese authorities. The large Manila Convent and College of the Sisters of the Assumption was the sisters' living quarters. Then, in July 1944, in an atmosphere of haste and secrecy, 2,100 people, 46 Maryknoll Sisters among them, were all moved by covered trucks and by train, to Los Baños Camp, about a two and a half hours' drive south of Manila. Housed in thatched-roofed, bamboo barracks with dirt floors, the prisoners lived crowded together in groups of seventy-five to one hundred, each with a total living space of three feet by seven feet. Primitive washing facilities and latrines were located in separate huts between the twenty-eight barracks, all surrounded by barbed wire, bamboo fences and eight guard towers. Although food was the most serious problem, the internees also suffered from water shortages and a lack of clothing.

Mother Mary Joseph's Ongoing Concern

During that fall of 1942, the light in Mother's room stayed on far into the night. At last alone after the demands of each full day, she was writing Christmas notes to all the sisters on the missions whom she had not been able to see the year before. It was not a new practice for her, but one which she had never done with such deliberate affection. That Christmas, she had to say and they had to receive some expression of the deep love that was in her heart for each of them.

Sister Mary Trinita Logue

On New Year's Day 1945, Sister Mary Trinita Logue, a fragile but indomitable figure, arrived into Los Baños Camp, on a crowded Japanese troop train from Manila. Covered with sores, with sunken eyes, unbelievably small, reduced to 78 pounds from her ordinary weight of a 160, she was able to walk, to smile and to put up her arms to embrace her sisters. In spite of surviving torture, water treatments, beatings and spending months in a hot, filthy dungeon, Sister M. Trinita appeared clear-headed and composed, happy to be with her sisters again. She had been released at last from Fort Santiago; she did not know how or why. No name had yet escaped her lips for the interrogators.

The Miracle

Observing American planes flying overhead was a punishable offense at Los Baños. A few minutes before 7 a.m., on February 23, 1945, as they were lining up for roll-call, the internees looked in astonishment at the gold-tinged sky. Floating across the hills were more than a hundred parachutes ~ *American Angels* who had come to rescue them. The challenge was to take the camp by surprise, disarm the Japanese and get the internees across *Laguna de Bay* to Manila before the Japanese Army was alerted. Such was the precision of the operation that there was not a single casualty among the internees or their rescuers.

The Return to Maryknoll

On March 9, 1945, twenty-one Maryknoll Sisters boarded the *S.S. Eberle* in Manila Bay. The ship was crowded, and they were instructed to stay below and wear their life jackets at all times. On May 2, they were reunited with their Maryknoll Sisters on the West Coast, debarking at San Pedro, California. On May 9, they were welcomed at Harmon Station by Mother Mary Joseph. She had planned to welcome all fifty-two sisters from the Philippines, but only twenty-one of them arrived in May 1945. Those who were physically more fit ~ or thought they were ~ stayed behind to begin again the works which the war had disrupted.

For the sisters, Mother put aside all the convent rules, including silence. They were, she told them, welcome to eat what they wanted when they wanted, to rest when their bodies asked for it, to talk when they had the inclination. At the end of a month, she felt they were ready to visit their homes, and that their appearance would no longer wring the hearts of their families as they had wrung hers.

Internment Camps in USA

Maryknoll Sisters had been serving the Japanese communities in Los Angeles, CA, and Seattle, WA, since 1920. The United States also had its own shameful internment camps. Fearing that Japan would recruit spies from ethnic Japanese living near the Pacific Coast, President Franklin D. Roosevelt issued Executive Order 9066 on February 19, 1942. It required all people of Japanese ancestry, United States citizens as well as Japanese citizens, to be interned inland in camps or confined to select places. With little notice, innocent Japanese families had to sell all they had, pack just a few suitcases, and go to poorly prepared camps hundreds of miles from their homes. Approximately 120,000 people were forcibly relocated; two-thirds were U. S. citizens, and half of them were children. The First Lady Eleanor Roosevelt wrote a letter to her husband expressing grave concerns for interning American Japanese, especially that the United States is a democracy.

The Executive Order permitted Japanese Sisters Mary Susanna Hayashi and Bernadette Yoshumochi to be interned at the Maryknoll Motherhouse in Ossining, NY, but they chose to accompany their parishioners to the Manzanar Internment Camp in California. From August 10, 1942, to October 28, 1945, these Maryknoll Sisters suffered the same hardships as the people they accompanied. In Seattle, WA, our Sisters Regina Johnson and Marie Rosaire Greaney, and other Maryknollers from Seattle and Los Angeles, visited their parishioners regularly in the camps.

A Reflective Moment
May our Maryknoll commitment
reflect a deeper, expansive, inclusive humanity,
where war is no longer an option.

Resources
The above Reflections were adapted from:
Maryknoll's First Lady by Jeanne Marie Lyons, MM;
Hearts on Fire by Penny Leroux;
A Pictorial History by Sister Mary Francis Louise, MM;
On the Threshold of the Future by Claudette LaVerdiere, MM;
As One Lamp Lights Another by Barbara Hendricks, MM;
Preaching by Living Justice by Bernice Kita, MM.

ᘓ ᘓ ᘓ

#22 ~ Some Events from 1944 to 1947

In 1945, Cardinal Cushing presented to Mother Mary Joseph an Honorary Doctor of Laws Degree from Regis College.

Mother Mary Joseph's First Honorary Degree

For the first time in its history, Regis College, a private Catholic Women's Liberal Arts College in Boston, MA, chose to honor *"one whose quiet unpublicized and hidden works are, in execution and effect, immense before God."* The one so honored was Mother Mary Joseph. On May 29, 1945, she was distinguished as *"the first Bostonian to found an American Community to prepare girls for missionary work."* She was cited *"for her courage and inspiring leadership, her keen insight and personal interest in her spiritual daughters....and for the universality of her zeal."* As was her wont, Mother saw only in this honor the achievement and acknowledgment of all her Maryknoll daughters with whom God had gifted her.

New Missions in Latin America

With the war still raging and missions closing in the Philippines, Japan, Korea and Manchuria, and imperiled in China, the sisters responded wholeheartedly to a new call in Latin America. Mother announced in March, 1943, the opening of a new mission in the Canal Zone. Sisters Lelia Makra from Manchuria, Socorro Maria Strong from the Philippines and Concepta Marie Brennan were chosen. Our mission work in Bolivia followed that same year, 1943, with Sisters Mercy Hirschboeck, Paula Sullivan, Kateri Peltier and Magdalen Mary McCloskey arriving to do medical and educational work. Their taxi at the airport was an oxcart.

At the request of the Capuchin Fathers, on September 24, 1944, six Maryknoll Sisters (Rose Anna Tobin, Elma Belscher, Marie Estelle Coupe, Kathleen Ryan, Margaret Patricia Walsh and Gonzaga Rizzardi) arrived in Managua, Nicaragua, to staff a school and clinic in Siuna. Their convent was not yet ready in Siuna, so they were welcomed by the Assumption Sisters, the very Community that had, on the other side of the world, protected our Maryknoll Sisters in the Philippines during the war years. Then on December 24, 1944, the sisters left Managua in a small propeller plane for the hour flight to Siuna. With great enthusiasm, they landed in a baseball field in the isolated jungle which was Siuna!

1946 ~ First Silver Jubilee

February 14, 1946, found Mother Mary Joseph with the first group of sisters to make vows, celebrating together their first twenty-five years as religious missioners. Many of them had been at Maryknoll much longer than twenty-five years and had formed the nucleus of the pioneer community.

Mother, who wrote a short letter about the event, looked forward to their Golden Jubilee with a hope *"to find that same mutual love which, to my mind, more than anything else, has brought so many blessings to the first twenty-five years of development. Our task on this anniversary day is unchanged. We have only to persevere in striving to know God's Will for us and in following it, allowing the Divine Builder to raise up or tear down, and without presumption on the one hand, or casting aside our weight of obligation, on the other, placing our all in God's keeping."*

The Fourth General Chapter
from July 13 to August 15, 1946

World War II had made deep inroads upon the lives of the Maryknoll Sisters. By the time the Fourth General Chapter was convened in 1946, Mother and the sisters had lived through a decade of war-torn mission experiences. It was almost ten years since the whole community had been able to come together to deliberate and make decisions *"to promote the family welfare."* Mother Mary Joseph announced that the General Chapter would begin on July 13, 1946. In her letter of convocation she pointed out the need to reorganize the work in order to meet the demands of reconstruction after the war. She was also keenly aware that this was a new historical moment filled with hope for a peaceful world and new possibilities in mission throughout the world. Maryknollers were challenged not only to reconstruct their missions in Asia but also to widen and deepen their mission vision in light of their overseas experience. Maryknoll had recently begun missions in Latin America and would soon turn to East Africa.

The Opening of the Chapter

In her introductory remarks, Mother stressed that the Congregation's spiritual beauty and ability to accomplish good works for God depended on the virtue and disciplined activity of each member. She quoted an entire talk given by Bishop Ford to the sisters in Kaying, China. He interpreted Father James A. Walsh's ideal qualities of the Maryknoll Sister, giving a vivid description of the four qualities most needed in a missionary context: simplicity with singleness of vision, unmeasured generosity, calm cheerfulness and forgetfulness of self. Mother was convinced that the holiness of each missioner sustained the entire missionary movement. As she spoke, the sisters could readily see this ideal Maryknoll Sister in the person of Mother.

Election of Mother Mary Joseph

In 1937, Mother had been elected to her third term in the form of a *postulation* ~ an exception allowed for a serious reason for a person to be Mother General beyond a second term of office. It was granted readily for Mother in 1937. The question raised now in 1946 by each of the sisters revolved around whether the Maryknoll Sisters were at point in time for a change in leadership. Mother was the first and only Mother General since her formal election in 1925. The sisters knew, and Mother noted, that she had been in the position long before then, in fact since 1912.

There were 23 delegates and the greater number of sisters thought of no one other than Mother Mary Joseph, even if it would be a fourth term for her. It was known also that Mother herself alone, and with her Councilors, had discerned deeply and decided that she would make herself available. She received 21 votes and again was elected in the form of a *postulation* which required canonical approval from Rome. Others elected were: Sister M. Paul McKenna, Vicaress; Sister M. Eunice Tolan; Sister M. Columba Tarpey, Sister M. Annette Kelley, Treasurer. Monsignor Nelson, Vicar for Religious of the Archdiocese of NY, was present for the elections as Cardinal Spellman's representative.

After study and discussion on the various proposed Chapter matters, the delegates made the required decisions, including Decennials (sisters returning for renewal every ten years). At the completion of their deliberations on August 15, 1946, Mother Mary Joseph prayed with the sisters as they returned to their mission fields.

Report of the 1946 Chapter

The experience of patient waiting for the canonical approval from Rome of Mother's *postulation* was a constant for every Maryknoll Sister and known well to her. She delayed sending the news of the Chapter hoping word, one way or the other, would come from Rome. Having that hope not realized, Mother took up her pen on October 26, 1946, and wrote:

> *I think I would want to write this letter myself anyway regardless of who might be #1.* She shared: *On the eve of the opening of Chapter, in the Chapel, before a Shrine in honor of the Immaculate Heart, the entire community being present, we placed the important event in the hands of Our Lady and then consecrated our Congregation to the Immaculate Heart of Mary.*

Mother outlined a report of the Chapter which covered the important decisions, indicating that the contents of the report were located also in the revised Constitutions and updated Directory which would soon be sent.

Simplifying Our Life of Prayer

At the Chapter Mother Mary Joseph had indicated that the time was ripe *"for simplifying our life of prayer and cultivating a true liberty of soul by which we may reach out at will towards God and not be hampered by an over-regimented parceled-out prayer life."* She recognized that the very heart of their religious life as a community was the Eucharist and the Divine Office. For those interned during the war, these had been *"the pearls of great price."* However, she had come to realize that mission life mandated occasions when the time available for prayer would be cut short by extenuating circumstances. In her letter she displayed both her trust in the integrity of each sister and her wisdom in regard to prayer, carefully delineating that her objective was to give each sister the responsibility of substituting a briefer prayer when necessary. It was characteristic of Mother to trust the sisters.

Refusal of the Postulation

In a meditative letter dated December 1, 1946, Mother communicated to the Congregation that Cardinal Spellman had sent for her on November 30 to speak about the *postulation*: *"He said he knows it will not be granted. If it were for a third term, there would be no difficulty, but not for a fourth term. He advised me to refuse the election and call an Elective Chapter. This, of course, I will do. While this act will take from my hands the government of the Congregation, it will also free me for things I have long wished to do and which should be of lasting help and benefit to us all."* Mother thanked the sisters for their love, their loyalty and their selfless cooperation from the beginning, adding that it had been an inexpressible joy to serve them. She and her Council called for the Elective Chapter to begin on January 2, 1947.

Natural Leaders in the Congregation

Two decades earlier, when the sisters were still a small group, the natural leaders had already begun to emerge, the most obvious being Sister M. Paul McKenna, the energetic Regional Superior from China. Another was Sister M. Columba Tarpey, who organized the sisters' mission in the Philippines and, after her return, served as Mother Mary Joseph's principal adviser, traveling to the missions and acting as Mother's stand-in at Ossining. But, though efficient administrators, neither was gifted with Mother's personal warmth. Sister M. Paul's strength was also her weakness, limiting her vision to the Orient, when China by the forties was only one part of the Maryknoll world, which had expanded to Latin America, and other parts of Asia. Sister M. Columba, on the other hand, was a builder with a global vision when Maryknoll was experiencing growth.

January 2, 1947 ~ Elective Chapter
Excerpts from Mother's Morning Meditation

This is the day which Our God has made. Let us rejoice and be glad therein! Every day in which we die to self and live unto Christ is a day of jubilation for us. Today is such a one. We can accept this change as a matter of simple obedience, or we can embrace it as an act of love....We must reach out to it, actively embracing it as God's evident will for us. So now in the sunshine of God's love, let us take a look at all there is to rejoice us on this day.

Mother's concluding words reverberate in the heart of every Maryknoll Sister:

Love, work, prayer, and suffering will sustain us in the future as they have in the past. All who are here now, all who will come after us will have no other tools than these with which to build....God had yet a great work for us to do....But the realization of this vision depends on you and me as individuals and on our cooperation. Do we love enough, do we work enough, do we pray enough, do we suffer enough? Maryknoll's future depends on our answer.

Sister M. Columba Tarpey Elected Mother General

Sister M. Columba Tarpey was elected the second Mother General, after which she was asked by the Cardinal's representative if she accepted. She stood for a moment facing the delegates without saying anything, her lips trembling and her eyes fastened on Mother Mary Joseph with entreaty, apology and sorrow. *"Take it, take it,"* said Mother Mary Joseph audibly, urgently. And when the obeisances to the new Mother General were made, Mother Mary Joseph was the first to make hers. As the Chapel resounded with the sound of the sisters' *Te Deum,* Mother watched with love as her sisters approached the altar and kissed the ring on the hand of a new Mother General. At the Elective Chapter, Sister Mary Coleman was chosen as one of the Councilors to take the place of Mother Mary Columba.

A Reflective Moment

Like Mother Mary Joseph, we are called to carry a great love
in our hearts, learning to go with the flow,
being stretched by the joys and difficulties of each new day.

Resources

The above Reflections were adapted from:
Maryknoll's First Lady by Jeanne Marie Lyons, MM;
To the Uttermost Parts of the Earth by Camilla Kennedy, MM;
Hearts on Fire by Penny Lernoux;
On the Threshold of the Future by Claudette LaVerdiere, MM;
Maryknoll History - A Pictorial History by Sister Mary Francis Louise, MM;
and Archival Material on Nicaragua and the 1946 Chapter.

80 80 80

Mother Columba Tarpey & Mother Mary Joseph.

Five Significant Events in Mother Mary Joseph's Life

*I*n response to a query for what constitutes
the most outstanding events of her life,
Mother Mary Joseph wrote the following letter
to Sister M. Columba Tarpey, dated December 17, 1946:

*I hardly know what to say, but perhaps
the following will do for what is wished:*

1. Going to Smith College where I saw the active work of Protestants for the missions. This led to my forming a mission study class at college; this was the immediate avenue of approach to Father Walsh to whom I wrote in October 1906, an event that marked the beginning of our friendship and our cooperation.

2. 1912 ~ Coming to Hawthorne and to Maryknoll.

3. 1914 ~ Visit to Europe with Miss Ward: In Rome received the impulse from the example of the 'Blue Nuns,' Nursing Sisters originally from England, who always had a sister praying for those especially out visiting the sick in their homes ~ to have similar adoration at Maryknoll. The Cloister and our adorations here are fruits of that.

4. Recognition of Rome ~ and after novitiate and sending of sisters to China ~ my first Mission Visitation.

5. Consecration and death of Father General with their profound effect on us and our growth. Love, Mother Mary Joseph

Mother Mary Joseph's Journey to the West Coast

From 1947 until the time of her death in 1955, Mother spent time in many different ways with the sisters. She thought of this time in her life as a call to a leadership of service *"in some new ways."*

Her first decision as Mother Founder was based on practical wisdom. She thought it best to leave the Motherhouse for a while, giving Mother Mary Columba the space and time to establish herself as the new leader of the Congregation. On February 5, 1947, almost one month to the day after Mother Mary Columba's election, Mother Mary Joseph expressed her desire to Mother Mary Columba to begin a journey to visit her large family of sisters without schedules to meet, but with time giving her and her sisters, leisure to enjoy each other.

In her new role in a community called to mission, Mother wanted to continue her work for the formation of her sisters. Despite her frequent periods of ill health, she wanted to be totally available to the sisters for their spiritual and human growth. She gave a retreat to the canonical novices, bade goodbye to all at Maryknoll and the New York Area, and then on February 11 left the Center going first to the West Coast accompanied by Sister James Rogers, her own sister. Here, they sojourned with the sisters on the Coast for a few months.

Valley Park, Missouri

Before the year visiting the sisters on the West Coast was finished, Mother had decided to respond to the constant urgings of Mother Mary Columba and the sisters to become part of a new Maryknoll venture ~ the establishment of a formation house for Maryknoll Sisters in Valley Park, Missouri. There was some apprehension in the community regarding how both the Maryknoll spirit and unity could be fostered and maintained away from the Motherhouse. Mother was very supportive of this project which was Mother Mary Columba's first major decision. Valley Park was large enough to receive at least half of the ninety-eight young women expected as candidates that year. Mother Mary Joseph wended her way across the country to Valley Park. She was aware that this was the first time that young women were to be trained as Maryknoll Sisters in a place other than at the Motherhouse.

Mother Mary Joseph arrived for the first time at Valley Park on October 10, 1947, and came upon the entrance sign, *Our Lady of Maryknoll Novitiate.* It was *"a profoundly moving moment."* She revealed the thoughts that touched her mind and heart: *"Had anyone read in my teacup that I would some day be living at a Maryknoll Sisters Novitiate in St. Louis, I would have believed it less easily that if the tea leaves had foretold a Novitiate residence in far off China. Yet here I am happy and privileged to be part of this new Maryknoll foundation."* Mother was *"at home"* immediately with the newest members *"of the newest branch of the old vine now deep-rooted in the Westchester hills"* at Maryknoll, NY.

Mother Mary Joseph Settles In

Mother was brought to her own quarters ~ two rooms which had once been the hospital supervisor's. These rooms had a lovely view of the Meramec Valley and were completely finished and furnished, a little haven of order and beauty in the great workshop that was the rest of the building. The next morning was one of great happiness. Archbishop Joseph Ritter, who had come to offer the first Mass, gave a little talk in which he recalled that October 7 was the anniversary of his arrival in St. Louis and that he looked upon this new house as an anniversary present to him from God. Without being asked, he blessed the building and, together with Monsignor Helmsing and Father John M. Martin, MM, stayed to breakfast with the sisters.

Mother Mary Joseph's Ingenuity

There were still many tasks to be done before the arrival of the young women candidates. Mother set to work finishing chests of drawers that needed to be assembled and then stained. This was not new to her; she had held a paint brush in her hand quite often in the early years at Maryknoll. She also offered to do the reading during meals in the refectory and sometimes helped prepare a meal. She turned her hand to most any task: playing the piano, planting daffodils, or cleaning the floors.

On her sixty-fifth birthday, October 27, 1947, she began the celebration by cooking a special breakfast. By the time the young women arrived, thirty-six on October 30 and twenty-one on the following day, Mother was an integral part of the small staff of sisters at the Valley Park Novitiate. She radiated the spark of love that always animated the community, calling forth harmony, self-gift, and spontaneous joy in those around her.

Mother invited the new postulants to drop in to see her whenever they were free, and especially if they felt homesick. They did, in threes and fours, sixes and sevens, sometimes in dozens! Sitting on her chairs, window seats and floor, they played her records, read her newspapers, listened to the football games which she turned on for them on the radio, emptied boxes of candy which she had on hand for them, and they let her have the benefit of their own views on life. They listened to her, too, and drank in her words thirstily.

Mother helped quicken the Maryknoll spirit to life for a new group of Maryknoll missioners. She recaptured the experiences of the early days in a slide show with her spontaneous running commentaries on each picture. Mother taught classes on Maryknoll history ~ a new venture for her. Last but not least, she meditated frequently with the sisters and gave annual retreats.

Mother Mary Joseph's Travels

Mother left Valley Park for the Motherhouse in early February 1948. Going back to the Motherhouse was a joy that she would never forget. However, upon arrival, she became quite sick with pneumonia accompanied by very high blood pressure. The convalescence period was long but, once back on her feet, she visited all the Maryknoll Sisters' houses on the east coast, then headed to Hawaii with Sister James. During her four months in Hawaii, she visited each of the eight missions established by her sisters on the Island of Oahu and two on Maui. In the fall of 1948 she settled in Monrovia, making it the center from which she visited all the missions in California. Wherever Mother went, she would become a part of the community willing to share her gifts whether these be domestic, artistic, intellectual or spiritual.

Mother Returns to the Motherhouse

By March 1949, Mother felt it was time for her to return to the Motherhouse to stay. Writing to Mother Mary Columba, she asked that she be allowed to have the chaplain's suite ~ two small rooms near the main chapel on the first floor. Mother Columba was delighted with this request, having the Mother Founder closer at hand for consultation on major concerns. Mother Mary Joseph did not intend to end her work but to undertake three writing projects that were constantly being urged on her: 1) The story of Maryknoll's beginnings, 2) the story of the Founders, and 3) her own vocation story.

In between the many calls on her time and energy, Mother tried to do these projects, but ultimately, all three would be left to Maryknoll posterity. By Christmas of 1949, Mother broke her silence of many months to send her Christmas greeting from the Motherhouse, the center and heart of Maryknoll where she had been happily ensconced for about seven months. In one line, she spoke volumes, *"How good it is to be home, no words can tell."* As she periodically gave meditations to the Community, Maryknoll Sisters taped her words for future generations.

New Missions

By 1947, the Communists were exerting control over more and more territory, and by 1950 all missioners in China were systematically arrested, imprisoned, and/or expelled. Korea faced the same upheaval and terror during the postwar years. The Maryknoll Sisters began to open missions in other areas. On September 21, 1948, Sisters Loretta Marie Hoffmann, Mary Camillus Reynolds and Andrew Marie McIver arrived on Koror, the chief Island in the Palau Group in the Caroline Islands. They started a grade school with the help of two Palauan girls who eventually entered the Mercedarian Novitiate.

In December 1948, Sisters M. Stanislaus Cannon, Margaret Rose Winkelmann, Joan Michel Kirsch and Catharine Maureen Bowes were headed for Tanganyika (now Tanzania) on the east coast of Africa, then a British Trust Territory under the United Nations. On December 27, 1948, the sisters arrived in Kowak near Lake Victoria in the northeast corner of Tanganyika.

On August 17, 1949, Sisters Madeline Maria Dorsey, Mary Bridgettine Mills, Paul Marie Gibbons, Kathleen Loretta Beyer, Mary Espiritu Venneman and M. Paul McKenna (sent with them to help start the work) arrived in Ceylon. A request came for sisters from the Ceylonese Government through Benedictine Bishop Bernard Regno of Kandy, Ceylon, to staff part of a 600 bed civil hospital.

On July 20, 1950, Sisters Mary Elvira Selgas, Thomas Marie (Regina) Johnson, Maria Carmen Fernandez and James Mary Scollan, went to Merida, Yucatan in Mexico.

On September 18, 1950, Sisters Marie Estelle Coupe and M. Petrona Litwin arrived in Galvarino, Chile.

On October 4, 1950, Sisters Andrew Marie McIver, M. Camillla Kennedy and Rose Patrick St. Aubin arrived in Likiep in the Marshall Islands where they worked with the Jesuits.

On March 30, 1952, Sisters Rose Jude Sharon and Bernard Mary Lowery began the mission in Lima, Peru. In 1954, Sister Rose Dominic Trapasso came from the diocesan social service agency in Honolulu to set up a Social Center in the new Maryknoll Parish of Santa Rosa in Lima, Peru. The Archbishop of Lima wanted this program extended throughout his diocese and asked Sister to handle the expansion.

On January 2,1953, Sisters Regina Johnson, M. Martina Bridgeman, Anna Maria Hartman and Mary Cabrini Gaudin arrived in Guatemala City, Guatemala, to begin mission work.

On November 17, 1953, Sisters Rita Marie Regan, Edith Rietz, Eileen Franz and Mary Cornelia Collins began our mission presence in Miaoli, Taiwan, and Sisters Antonia Maria Guerrieri, Dominic Marie Turner and Josephine Marie Isaac in Taichung/Changhua, Taiwan.

Faithful Promoters on the Road

In January 1948, Sisters Eleanor Hogan and Henry (Agnes) Josberger called on a pastor in Somerville, MA. That Monsignor, though a fine priest, was not exactly mission generous. Alighting from a trolley car, they trudged to the rectory between snow banks more than three feet high on a sub-zero morning. The pastor greeted the sisters kindly and asked how they got there. When he heard that it was by street car and *shanks mare* (walking), he was impressed by their spirit, but he did not give them a date for a collection at the parish. He did offer them a cup of hot coffee before they left. Many minutes later, the sisters were still standing at the corner waiting for the trolley, and the pastor came and invited them back to the rectory. He then went into another room and came back with a four-digit check!

A Reflective Moment

Mother Mary Joseph knew that we advance toward our destiny
when we encourage others to reach theirs!

Resources

The above Reflections were adapted from:
Maryknoll's First Lady by Jeanne Marie Lyons, MM;
To the Uttermost Parts of the Earth by Camilla Kennedy, MM;
On the Threshold of the Future by Claudette LaVerdiere, MM;
Maryknoll Sisters, A Pictorial History by Sister Mary Francis Louise, MM;
As One Lamp Lights Another by Barbara Hendricks, MM;
Distaff (Sisters Diary) by
Eunice Tolan, MM, and Incarnata Farrelly, MM;
and Archival Material regarding the opening of new missions.

ജ   ജ   ജ

Mother Mary Joseph with Ms. Elizabeth Deering Hanscom (left) in June 1950 at Smith College when Mother received an Honorary Degree.

#24 ~ Mother Mary Joseph's Last Years

Honorary Degree by Smith College

During the year 1950, Smith College offered Mother Mary Joseph an honorary degree. This was the third time that Smith had made such an offer. Her acceptance of an honorary degree from Regis College, Boston, on May 29, 1945, or from Trinity College, Washington, D.C., on November 5, 1949, had presented no difficulty. They were Catholic institutions. Smith was not. The first invitation by Smith was in 1940, but the Bishop of Springfield, MA, had asked Mother to refuse. Needless to say, she found it a bit awkward to refuse the honor. God had used Smith College as the instrument through which her vocation to foreign mission work materialized and, naturally, it had a warm place in her heart. In February of 1943, Smith sent a second invitation but Mother, being quite ill at the time, refused this one. To be invited a third time in 1950 was startling indeed and Mother did not know how she could go about refusing it, nor did she want to. It was thought that the new Bishop-elect of Springfield, Massachusetts, might see things in a different light than his predecessor. He did and gave permission readily. June 1950 was also the 45ᵗʰ anniversary of Mollie's graduation from Smith College.

Citation Accompanying the Degree of Doctoris Letterarum Humaniorum Awarded to Mother Mary Joseph by Smith College ~ June 3, 1950

The citation speaks clearly of Mother Mary Joseph's place
in the life of American Women Religious in the Catholic Church:

Mother Mary Joseph (Mary Josephine Rogers, 1905 Graduate) *has been named one of the first ladies (Religious Sisters) of the Catholic Church in America to receive an honorary degree from Smith. As a young woman her faith inspired a sense of dedication to humanity and a clear vision for translating that dedication into the service of humankind. She founded the first American Community of Catholic Foreign Mission Sisters.*

She guided this Order of Maryknoll Missioners during a third of a century and has helped to mold it into a great organization which extended the Christian faith and provided material aid to thousands of unnamed people throughout the Orient, the Pacific Islands, Latin America, Africa, and among people in the United States.

Mother Mary Joseph at the Motherhouse

Mother Mary Columba was away from the Motherhouse in 1951 visiting the Maryknoll Sisters throughout the world, those who could be reached during the Communist takeover in China. Meanwhile, at Maryknoll, Mother Mary Joseph was involved in all that concerned the sisters and the work of the Community. In the spring of 1951, she began to get news of the sisters in South China as they crossed the border into Hong Kong, a few at a time. Each sister carried the story of communist hostility and accusations; some had endured long weeks under house arrest. Several had suffered frightful days and nights in communist prisons.

In April, news reached Hong Kong that Bishop Francis X. Ford with his secretary, Sister Joan Marie Ryan, had been arrested. By winter it was obvious that, at this moment of history, the Maryknoll Missions, as well as all other Christian missions, were coming to a tragic end in China. While her growing Congregation of women missioners was spreading out in Latin America and Africa, Mother Mary Joseph realized that their missions in China were being destroyed. Mother held these experiences of joy and suffering together in her heart continually reminding her sisters to pray for those in danger.

Mother Mary Joseph's Wheelchair Chauffeur

Sister Cabrini Gaudin, from the first group of postulants at Valley Park Novitiate, who knew Mother well, was appointed her wheelchair chauffeur. She shared with Mother that she was surprised to be given this task, as she never seemed to be able to guide any moving vehicle! Mother said laughingly, *"Oh fate! We will manage. You push and I will guide!"* They sailed through the long ambulatory, made a sharp left turn into the back of chapel, resumed speed, and crashed into the holy water font. It rocked back and forth and splashed Mother with holy water. Mother blessed herself with the water and remarked, *"Stopping for holy water was to have come in the second lesson!"* Thereafter, when her chauffeur, looking apologetically, came to her door with the wheelchair, Mother would greet her with a cheerful, *"The chariot of Elias and the driver thereof!"*

Mother's Serious Illness

The wheelchair was not sufficient concession to the disabilities which plagued Mother Mary Joseph ~ high blood pressure and fibrillating heart, and the nagging diabetes. On March 23, 1952, she suffered a severe stroke that was further complicated by her medical history. Paralyzed on the left side, her rich voice reduced to a broken, struggling whisper, she was completely bedridden at first. As she regained some strength, she set herself to the long task of rehabilitation, determined to walk again, to recover as much motion and usefulness as possible. She was ready to follow the exacting routine and often exhausting exercises which this demanded. There was nothing grim about her determination, however, and whether she was in her room at the Motherhouse or at the hospital, an atmosphere of good cheer, of normality, of optimism, surrounded her. However, after long months of therapy, coupled with a determined spirit, she regained enough motion to sit in a wheelchair and enjoy a tour of the Maryknoll compound, but she was not able to walk again.

In September, 1952, the news reached Mother that Sister Joan Marie Ryan had arrived in Hong Kong with the heartrending story of Bishop Ford's death in the prison at Canton. This was one of the most painful messages that Mother received during the Communist takeover of the Asian missions. Francis Xavier Ford had been the first seminarian to arrive at Hawthorne in 1912 and, like many of the early seminarians, he considered Mother to be his spiritual mother, which indeed she was.

Wheelchair Excursions

Although in September, 1952, Mother was herself reflecting on the possibility of imminent death and reunion with *"Maryknoll-in-heaven,"* by the end of the year she had regained enough strength and mobility to sit in a wheelchair. For Christmas the sisters at the Motherhouse had made a new outdoor crib. Mother had seen some of the figures before they were placed. This gave her an idea which she tried out half-jokingly on Mr. Potter, the engineer. *"I would like to see that crib,"* she said. *"Do you think you and Joe could get me, in my wheelchair, into the truck and drive me there?"* Mr. Potter digested the idea. *"Well, sure,"* he agreed. Once up the improvised board ramp and into the truck, Mother looked out of her blankets to say, *"Now that we are out, we might just as well continue up the hill and see the sisters at the Cloister."* They went and Mother was a sensation! For the next three years Mother would continue to share actively with her Maryknoll Family.

Mass in Mother Mary Joseph's Room

The Vicar for Religious, Monsignor Joseph Nelson, gave permission for Mother to have Mass said in her room. There was space for half a dozen others and little notes went out to the sisters in turn, inviting them to fill these places. After Mass, each would go to her beside for a greeting and a kiss. When Mother had improved enough to be helped in and out of a car, she went as far as the Venard Convent in Pennsylvania and the new Novitiate at Topsfield, MA, which opened in 1953.

At St. Vincent's Hospital in NYC

When Mother was at St. Vincent's Hospital in New York City for a rehabilitation program during November and part of December of 1954, the whole staff enjoyed working with her. She was always eager to begin the day, ready to try whatever was suggested, unafraid and trustful, unfailingly good-tempered.

One day she was on the elevator with her nurse and another Maryknoll Sister. A well-dressed woman got on and, looking at the three of them, said, "*Oh, you are Maryknoll Sisters. I used to know your order years ago. Whatever happened to that great big ~ oh, she was a very big woman ~ who started the whole thing?*" A small silence fell. Mother did not let it lengthen. She could never bear to have anyone embarrassed. She pointed to herself, smiling: "*I'm it,*" she said, "*guilty on all counts!*"

Being Weighed

During this rehabilitation program, Mother had to be weighed daily. She could not stand on an ordinary scale and her nurse used to take her by wheelchair to the kitchen commissary. There she was weighed on the meat scale, one of the kitchen personnel assisting! She and her nurse used to laugh together over the ignoble implications in this procedure.

One day Mother said, "*Don't we pass the morgue on the way to the kitchen? I have always wanted to see the inside of a morgue. Let's go in.*" They went in. "*There's a scale,*" Mother exclaimed. "*All you have to do is roll the wheelchair on it. Then you can weigh it separately when I get back to bed. That will be much easier for you than helping that man get me on and off the other one.*" "*You are really the smartest Mother in the world,*" said her nurse. "*Oh, no, I'm not,*" said Mother, laughing, "*I was reading about the city morgue in my detective story last night. That's how the thought came to me!*"

Mother Mary Joseph's Awareness of Others

Mother was just as aware of those around her in the hospital as she was at home. She noticed that a priest, who was also a wheelchair patient, looked shabby. *"He may not have any people still living,"* she said. *"You must go out and buy him some shirts and pajamas."* Sister Mary de Paul Cogan, who had been closely associated with Mother since the early twenties and who had always had a special place in her affections, died in November 1953 at the Motherhouse. When told of this, Mother said nothing but sat silently for some time. Then she asked that arrangements be made for her to return to the Motherhouse for the funeral. She then quietly took up again the book which she had been reading. That evening Sister Rose Assunta Buell ventured to express her sympathy. Mother answered, *"Yes, she wanted me to be there and, had I known, I would have been. But I was where God wanted me and it does not matter now."*

Mother's Beautiful Character

All her life Mother Mary Joseph had shielded people who brought her hardship and grief, not only those who loved her but also those who opposed or rejected her. It was an old habit with her. At Smith her classmates had become conscious of it during the year that she roomed with a girl who was, they thought, odd. *"How do you stand her? You know she's queer, Mollie."* Mollie responded, *"She's different. We're not all alike."* Through the years, the heaviest crosses that others laid upon her shoulders she shared with no one unless for one reason or another she had to do so. If age or the failures and the crosses in one's life could not dry up the deep well of Mother's heart, neither could illness accomplish it. As soon as she was well enough, she let it be known that every sister who arrived at the Motherhouse or who left it for some mission was welcome to come to see her. To her room, too, were invited the large groups of entering postulants whom she delighted to see. Her gratitude and affection overflowed on others in whatever means and opportunities were still available to her. These might be only a look, a greeting, an invitation to come to see her, a small gift or one of her little notes.

Becoming a Pontifical Institute

Mother first mentioned to Father James A. Walsh in 1923 the advisability that we become a Pontifical Institute. This was not followed through until the 1952 General Chapter, when the decision was taken to apply for Pontifical status in early 1953. On December 12, 1954, the Maryknoll Sisters Congregation became a Pontifical Institute. At that time, the title of the Congregation was officially changed from Foreign Mission Sisters of St. Dominic to Maryknoll Sisters of St. Dominic.

Ten years later, on September 5, 1964, at the request of the Maryknoll Sisters, the Maryknoll Society's Superior General, Bishop John W. Comber, authorized the Maryknoll Sisters to use the initials *MM* after their names, stating: *"After discussing it with the members of the Council, I wish to assure you that there will be no objection from us."*

Spring 1955

Spring had never seemed more beautiful at Maryknoll than in 1955. Mother was out as much as possible and missed nothing. She had a way of putting out her good hand in a gesture that seemed to encompass and pay tribute to all nature ~ violets, daffodils, budding maples, evergreens, sky. *"Perfectly beautiful!"* she would say. She would sit watching the sisters gardening, whether they planted or weeded. She was particularly interested in a section then being developed called *Sarto Garden* in honor of St. Pius X, who was canonized in 1954. To this she contributed a number of plants, including dozens of petunias, remarking, *"They require so little attention and contribute so much ~ like sisters in community!"* Sarto Garden is near the Chalet driveway where the two trees named *Justice and Peace* are kissing (Ps. 85).

A Reflective Moment

Through her journey of illness, Mother came to realize
that any sickness or aging is part of our love journey with God,
and is at the heart of our mission-contemplative charism,
surrendering ourselves to the great Mystery of Love.

Resources

The above Reflections were adapted from:
Maryknoll's First Lady by Jeanne Marie Lyons, MM;
To the Uttermost Parts of the Earth by Camilla Kennedy, MM;
On the Threshold of the Future by Claudette LaVerdiere, MM;
As One Lamp Lights Another by Barbara Hendricks, MM;
and Archival Material.

ℴ☙ℴ☙ℴ☙

October 3, 1955
Mother with Lily Windsor.

#25 ~ Mother Mary Joseph's Last Days

As the summer of 1955 wore on, those around Mother noticed that she seemed increasingly tired, preoccupied and almost uninterested in what was going on. This was unlike her, but it did not last long. On the third of October, Mother visited the Contemplative Community on the hill. The sisters had invited her to celebrate their twenty-third anniversary, and she spent the entire morning with them and dinner at noon. That evening Mother Mary Joseph joined the Motherhouse community at a concert by the well-known singer, Lily Windsor, whose beautiful voice and delightful humor she always enjoyed. She stayed for the whole program.

Mother and Sister M. John Cahill
The next day, October 4, Mother took her regular period of adoration in the chapel from twelve-thirty to one-thirty in the afternoon. Gentle Sister John Cahill, one of the dwindling 1921 first profession group, wanted to see Mother. The nurse brought Mother to the infirmary, where Sister John was ill. They talked about Maryknoll's early days, about its growth, and other blessed memories. Back in her room and encouraged to take a nap, Mother found it hard to settle down, wanting to change her position frequently. In the evening, however, she seemed quite herself and received a brief visit from Cardinal Gracias of Bombay, India, together with Monsignor Jeffers of the New York Archdiocese, Bishop Lane, MM and Father McCarthy, MM.

Mother Mary Joseph Taken to the Hospital
On October 5, Mother joined a small group of sisters celebrating the departure of a sister about to leave for her first mission. Mother had suffered two attacks of nausea before the dinner was over, becoming very weak, with chills and perspiration. The next morning, Thursday, October 6, she said that she had had the best night in many and was soon up in her favorite chair, reading her mail and the newspapers.

However, on October 7 during the night, she experienced alarming symptoms and it was soon decided to arrange for a room at St. Vincent's Hospital in New York City. Mother Columba alerted her Council and those sisters who would go with Mother Mary Joseph, including Mother's own sister, Sister James Rogers. She arranged with Father David I. Walsh, MM, Local Superior at the Seminary, to come for the anointing of the Sacrament of the Sick which took place just before the Ambulance Service arrived early Saturday morning, October 8. When the men came to carry her to the ambulance, Mother did not want them to think that they had to be excessively careful with her. "*These sisters,*" she said, smiling at the nurses, "*move me around like a sack of potatoes.*" On the way to St. Vincent's Hospital she said to one of the sisters, "*Give the attendants a tip, and more than enough for a cup of coffee.*" Arriving at the hospital, she remembered that Sister Kevin Hayes was there after having had some minor surgery. "*I would like to go to see Sr. Kevin,*" she said, "*Later, Mother, when you feel better.*"

Surgery Performed

During the morning it was decided that surgery should be attempted. With it, Mother might have a chance. She was taken to the operating room. In all too short a while Mother Columba was called. The surgeon, Dr. Louis M. Rousselot, expressed his sorrow, explaining that there was generalized peritonitis, probably due to a mesenteric clot and an almost completely gangrenous condition. The doctor said, "*I do not believe she will last twelve hours, and I think it will run down faster than that.*" Mother had block anesthesia and was fully conscious when Mother Columba went to the operating room. When Mother Columba put her hand on Mother Mary Joseph's arm, Mother greeted her with words which were typical of her response to life. "*I'm fine,*" she said, "*everything will be all right.*"

Both before and after the operation, young Dr. W. Marshall East, who assisted Dr. Rousselot, remarked that Mother's subjective and even her objective symptoms did not seem reconcilable with her serious physical condition. An hour later Mother Mary Joseph was removed from the recovery room, and taken back to her room. Conscious and alert, she greeted those around her, smiling in her usual manner despite two tubes inserted in her nostrils, providing her with oxygen and drainage.

Mother's Last Moments

Sister Teresa Marie Viveiros who had been Mother's secretary and now Mother Columba's, had informed Mother Mary Joseph's family and friends that she was now in her final hours. By Saturday afternoon, October 8, many began to visit and pray at her bedside.

The Superior General Bishop Raymond Lane, was among these visitors; he recited the prayers for the dying and gave Mother the Apostolic Blessing. Monsignor Nelson and Maryknoll Fathers and Sisters and Mother's own relatives also visited. Mother Mary Columba remained close to her bedside and Sister James was near at hand saying one Rosary after another.

Early Saturday evening two cars arrived from Maryknoll, bringing a number of Maryknoll Sisters and Father Anthony Cotta, the Motherhouse chaplain. They gathered around Mother's bed, praying and singing the traditional hymn, *Salve Regina*. By Sunday afternoon Mother found it hard to speak and finally managed a halting indistinct, *"How are you?"* to Dr. Samuel S. Sverdlik, whom she greatly admired and liked. She did not speak again. It did not matter. What was left for her to say to those to whom her mind and heart had always been open, to whom she had spoken not in words but in a thousand tellings which only love could devise?

Reflecting the consistent humility and faith Mother had throughout her life, her last request through one of her nurses, Sister Rose Assunta Buell, was: *"Please tell Mother Columba to ask the sisters to pray for me. They will think I do not need prayers, but I do."* When Father Cotta, the Motherhouse Chaplain, her friend and confessor and informal photographer for many years, arrived, he could hardly believe that she who had always admired his pictures and laughed at his jokes could be unconscious of his presence. *"She does not know that I am here,"* he said sorrowfully. *"She doesn't know."*

Mother's Death

Mother Mary Columba described the moment of Mother's passing very simply: *"We all prayerfully waited for God's call, which came quietly after a few short struggles for breath at 5:18 p.m."* Mother Mary Joseph Rogers died on Sunday, October 9, 1955. However, as long as there is a Maryknoll Sister left in the world with a heart to love and a will to serve, Mother's life, spirit and mission continues on this sacred earth!

The Three Founders' Formal Resolve

Forty-five years earlier, on September 10, 1910, at the 1st Eucharistic Congress in Montreal, Fathers James A. Walsh and Thomas F. Price had agreed to work together for the foundation of a foreign mission seminary in the USA. One week later, on September 15, 1910, Mollie Rogers had made a formal resolve to devote her entire life to the foreign mission initiative that would soon become known as Maryknoll. Over those many years she had given herself entirely ~ body, mind, heart and soul ~ to the foundation of this missionary movement, the first of its kind among Catholics in the USA.

Mother's Gifts to Her Daughters

One of Mother's outstanding gifts during her many years of leadership was the profoundly spiritual yet deeply human formation for mission that she gave the Maryknoll Sisters. She often described what she called the Maryknoll Spirit as naturalness of manner, frankness and openness. For her sisters she put forth this ideal: *"I would have her distinguished by Christ-like charity, a limpid simplicity of soul, heroic generosity, selflessness, unfailing loyalty, prudent zeal, gracious courtesy, an adaptable disposition, solid piety, and the saving grace of a kindly humor."* The Maryknoll Spirit is not only an ideal guiding the Maryknoll Sisters; it is also an unending challenge to grow in the compassionate love of Jesus, sharing faith, hope and love among the peoples of all nations.

Mother made her sisters a *family,* more through her own capacity as their Mother than through any instruction. She shared with them the beloved burden of her responsibilities as well as the recognition that sometimes came to her, and she had more than once reminded them it was together that they had done something for God. Together, the sisters were encouraged to form a strongly bonded community of apostolic women, wholly committed to the following of Jesus in his mission to the world. As a gracious guide with a unique vision of the mission vocation, she enjoined each sister to be responsible for the common good of the whole Congregation, *saying: "If you love Maryknoll....you will put aside self-love and self-interests....and you will give to one another that beautiful gift, especially charity."* Mother carefully shaped this Maryknoll Spirit through her conferences and letters, the reading she encouraged, and her own relationships with the sisters, being wont to quote, *"As one lamp lights another, nor grows less, so nobleness enkindles nobleness."*

Mother's Heritage

Mother Mary Joseph was the last of the three Maryknoll Founders. By the time of her death in 1955, the Maryknoll Sisters' Congregation had 1,160 members. There had been an average net increase of 32 sisters a year for the previous thirty-five years. At this point Maryknoll Sisters had established 84 missions in Asia: Hong Kong, Korea, the Philippines, Japan, Ceylon and Taiwan; in Africa: Tanzania and Mauritius; in the Pacific Islands: Hawaii, the Marshall Islands and the Caroline Islands; in Latin America: Bolivia, Panama, Nicaragua, Guatemala, Mexico, Chile and Peru. Over a thirty-five year span from 1920 to 1955, the Maryknoll Sisters had also opened missions in the United States among the Japanese, Chinese, Latin American and African American communities.

Cardinal Spellman

Close to eleven o'clock in the evening on October 9, the day Mother Mary Joseph died, Mother Mary Columba received a telephone call from Cardinal Spellman, Archbishop of New York. He expressed his sympathy for the Maryknoll Sisters in the death of Mother Mary Joseph and then asked if he might celebrate a Pontifical Requiem for Mother's funeral at the Motherhouse. His closing words gave great consolation to Mother Mary Columba and the sisters. *"I had great respect and admiration for her (Mother Mary Joseph) and this is the first time I have offered to say a Pontifical Mass."*

A Reflective Moment

After Mother Mary Joseph's death, many letters of appreciation came to the Motherhouse.
Below are excerpts from a few letters:

Her spirit has so permeated each sister that Maryknoll will never truly be without Mother Mary Joseph.

History will never be correctly written unless it includes her glorious name!

Her grand spirit, which is the soul of your community, belongs to all of us.
(From a Society of the Propagation of the Faith Director)

Mother Mary Joseph became a worldwide figure of such great stature that all Nations will call her blessed!

Resources

The above Reflections were adapted from:
Maryknoll's First Lady by Jeanne Marie Lyons, MM;
On the Threshold of the Future by Claudette LaVerdiere, MM;
As One Lamp Lights Another by Barbara Hendricks, MM;
and 1955 Archival Material.

ЄꙨ   ЄꙨ   ЄꙨ

#26 ~ Mother Columba's Letter Regarding the Death of Mother Mary Joseph

Feast of Mater Admirabilis
October 20, 1955

My dear Sisters,

It is with a deep consciousness of your eagerness for details of our Mother Mary Joseph's last days that I shall try to recount something of them for you. Through the thoughtful arrangements of Sister Jeanne Marie Lyons, I am writing in a *burrow* at *Regina Maris* in Noroton, CT, a spot beloved by Mother, a sojourn at which often accorded her a new lease on life. My heart goes out to each and all of you in this greatest and poignant sorrow. As no doubt with you, our emotions are mixed as we mourn our personal loss combined with a sense of Mother's spiritual presence and of her already evident new awareness of all our interests and trials.

Although from the time Mother suffered a series of cerebral accidents while returning from the wake of Father McGuane, pastor of Noroton, CT, on Passion Sunday, March 23, 1952, we at home daily dreaded the inevitable aftermath. We were hardly prepared for the manner of her going and the suddenness of it. Mother was a constant inspiration to all in the way she struggled courageously and valiantly, to the ultimate of her physical strength, to participate in all Community ceremonies and celebrations. She shielded us from concern by an ever ready assurance that she was fine. We kept her abreast of all important happenings, sparing her whatever we could of a worrisome nature as far as possible. The following is a composite of my own, the doctors and the Sister-nurses observations during the recent months.

With a heart condition of long standing, Mother's strength was always taxed by hot muggy days. On the whole the past summer was comfortable, but there was a period of over two weeks of sustained record-breaking high temperature.

During August, Mother, Sister James and the nurses went by car to Vermont where they saw the Trapp Family Estate and remained a few days at a comfortable nearby Motel. This was a blessed relief, but on her return and as August drew to a close, we became aware of Mother's waning strength and of her withdrawal of interest in passing visitors and events from time to time.

In looking back, the nurses and we who saw her daily, believe this marked the time of the onset of the hidden process which caused her death ~ peritonitis from gangrenous intestines resulting from clots in the mesenteric aorta. During the second week of August, Mother began to have pain in her back, radiating to the left thigh. Upon physical examination, the doctors diagnosed it as an old stand-by arthritis present in its acute stage. The potent drug did not have the desired effect and was discontinued after four days.

Mother's nights were poor. It was decided to take her to Regina Maris for two or three days, thinking it might do her good. She went Thursday, September 29, and returned home Saturday looking rested and more like herself. On Thursday, October 3, Mother was invited by our Contemplative Community for their twenty-third anniversary dinner. Sister Regina Therese and Sister Michael Maureen accompanied her and I drove them up to and through the garden gate; promising to return for her at 2:30. Mother apparently suffered no ill-effect from the dinner and was able to enjoy her visit with her contemplative daughters until three o'clock. Sister Theodore had group pictures taken with Mother, which must have been an inspiration from the Holy Spirit.

We returned home by way of the service entrance so that Mother could survey and inspect the progress of the new wing. Mother rested until supper time and was ready for the evening concert by Lily Windsor. She enjoyed hearing Lily very much and though she tired easily, she bravely stayed till the end.

On Monday and Tuesday mornings the nurses had Mother sleep until late and we cancelled her Mass for the two days. On Wednesday, after the inspiring talk by Cardinal Gracias of Bombay, India, in the Novices' Chapel, Sister Regina Therese went back and gave Mother a brief account of the Cardinal's message and especially mentioned the high praises he bestowed on Mother, and how fortunate we were to have the Founder in our midst. Thursday, when Sister Michael Maureen, just back from her pre-departure home visit, received word from home that her brother's wife and the mother of five children, the youngest six weeks old, had died suddenly that morning, Mother was very much concerned and became upset over the news. She was most anxious to have Sister Michael Maureen return home.

Two Sisters drove her home. That evening, while we were all gathered together for a departure supper and games in the Bishop's Suite, Mother began the first acute stage of her final illness. It marked the beginning of three days of suffering for Mother Mary Joseph.

She seemed to enjoy the first course, chicken pie, etc., but a few minutes after six o'clock, Sister Ann Geraldine, who had driven Sister Michael Maureen home, returned and Mother lost no time in finding out what had happened to Sister's sister-in-law. She was twenty-five years of age and died of a coronary embolism.

Mother calmly proceeded with her supper. She was nauseated just before dessert was served and the nurses wheeled her into the bathroom, not too alarmed at this time for it was not unusual for Mother to lose a meal since she had that esophageal hernia. After her dessert she was again nauseated and was taken into the bathroom. While there Mother complained to her nurses of feeling weak. She was cold and began to perspire profusely with all the clinical signs of shock, so, without returning, they hurried Mother back to her room. No sooner had they gotten Mother into bed, she lost all her supper.

Sister Lois was a departure guest, due to leave the next morning. She was called to Mother's room and was able to check on her acute condition. Mother's blood pressure was above 260 systolic and she was showing signs of shock and acidosis with a great possibility of another vascular "accident."

Sister Lois returned to the Bishop Suite to ask if Sister Paula Therese could be called in to recheck Mother's condition. Sister Paula Therese before entering had a fine experience of seven or eight years at Duke Hospital where they conduct a special study of high blood pressure and arterio sclerosis. From here on, the medical team did their best to relieve Mother's critical condition and Friday Mass was cancelled.

Mother had a poor night and on Friday, Feast of the Holy Rosary, the nurses felt she must have offered herself to Our Lady. Friday morning as they were trying to make Mother comfortable, she asked if they had any gift to give Sister Mary Rhoda on her feast day. In the evening she inquired about Mr. Potter whom she thought had a physical checkup and was concerned about it. Her mind was constantly on someone and far removed from her own critical condition ~ never any *organ recitals*. She accepted all discomfort with a happy resignation.

All day Friday Sister Paula Therese checked closely and gave medical treatment according to the laboratory tests. The vomiting persisted all day and late in the afternoon they noticed the first clinical sign, abdominal distention with a possibility of obstruction in the abdominal cavity. Sister Paula Therese suspected and feared a mesenteric clot. Not being able to retain any fluid, Mother became very dehydrated and intravenous fluid was given to restore the balance in her tissues. Sister Paula Therese, Sister Philip Marie, night nurse, and Sister Regina Therese did all they could to alleviate Mother's acute condition, and after 2:30 a.m. were at a standstill.

Sister Paula Therese decided to wait for a while and pray about it. Shortly after 3:00 a.m., she came up to my room and gave a very anxious report on Mother's serious condition. The diabetes had been out of control but a balance had been established. Sister was alarmed by the abdominal distension, the blood pressure which was at 300, temperature at 103, the pulse and respiration rising. Sister Justin had just run off a blood count with the alarming result of 30,000 white cells. Sister Paula Therese was deeply concerned and worried. She thought we should get Mother to a hospital without delay where the benefit of consultation and facilities were available.

We tried to get the doctors without success, but I called up St. Vincent's in New York City and Sister Paula Therese spoke to the night supervisor who assured us she would have a room. I telephoned Father David I. Walsh, Local Superior at the Seminary, about having Mother anointed and then requested an ambulance from the Peekskill Ambulance Service. Through the buzzer to Sister Teresa Marie's room, I was able to ask her to alert the Council, the house Superiors and Sister James. Father Walsh gave Mother a particle of the Host as Viaticum and then gave Holy Communion to those who were going to the Hospital with Mother. By 5:20 a.m., we were on our way with Sister Teresa Marie trying to follow the ambulance but, with no impeding traffic at that hour, they must have maintained a speed of 65 miles and we were outdistanced.

The young resident physician, Doctor O'Connor, was with Mother, so the three in the Mercury vehicle went down to 6:30 a.m. Mass and there we saw Sister Edward Marie, our student nurse, and broke the startling news to her. Sister Marian Catherine, Superintendent of Nurses, took us all to the cafeteria for breakfast and added her personal service. She released our student to join the others with Mother. The Superior, Sister Loretto Bernard, came to tell us she was assigning to our use Room 1004 with a lavatory on the floor above Mother's which she thought would be nicer than the public waiting alcove.

After breakfast I spoke to Doctor O'Connor who said he called Doctor Kennedy (to whom Doctor Sverdlik had referred Mother last summer) and he would be in between 9:00 and 9:30 a.m., so we continued to wait on Mother's floor near her room 912. It was 10:00 a.m. before he arrived and after examining Mother, he came out looking very serious. The sisters introduced me and he said, "*Mother is in a grave condition. There is peritonitis due to one of three causes ~ diverticulitis, hiatus hernia, or mesenteric clot. I doubt if Mother could stand surgery, but a surgical consultation is indicated. Have you any one in mind?*" I replied that we knew a couple of doctors on the staff but not in that field, so Doctor Kennedy said he would call someone ~ who later turned out to be Doctor Rousselot, Chief of Surgery, formerly of Columbia.

Sister Stella Marie had come over with Sister Edmund Damien, so she invited us to Chinatown for dinner. Dear Sister Teresa Marie was kept busy trying to telephone, for she had been unable to reach Mother's niece, Ellen (Mrs. Bond). Sister Charles in her usual generous way hurried dinner for 12:00 noon instead of 12:30 and just as we were about to sit down, they telephoned from St. Vincent's to say Mother was being booked for surgery at 1:30 p.m., as she had a fifty-fifty chance. Sister Teresa Marie with Sister Stella Marie as companion took Sister Paula Therese and me without delay to the hospital and they returned to Chinatown for Sister James, stopping enroute to tell Ellen Bond in person of Mother's impending surgery. Sisters Regina Therese and Ann Geraldine arrived about this time. The interns and nurses were busy with preliminaries in Mother's room, including cardiogram, so that it was 2:00 p.m. when Mother was taken to the operating Room #1 on the same floor. I telephoned home to ask that telegrams and cables be sent to our houses alerting all to the gravity of Mother's condition. In the meantime Ellen had arrived and offered to phone the relatives. We all repaired to Room 1004 and continued saying Rosaries.

After 2:30 p.m. Sister Edward Marie came to our room, wearing her operating room mask, to say they wanted me in surgery. My heart sank and I hurried after her down the fire escape fearing Mother had died on the table. The Superior, Sister Loretto Bernard, the Superintendent of Nurses and Sister Supervisors were looking through the glass door of the operating room to which they beckoned me. Sister Rose Assunta, Regina Therese, Edward Marie and Paula Therese had all been permitted to attend, and when the latter sighted me, she came out exclaiming in great distress, "*Oh, it's awful! I never saw such an involved condition. The intestines are completely gangrenous from stomach to rectum; clotting in the mesenteric aorta. They can do nothing.*"

As they finished, Doctor Rousselot came out to me and expressed his sorrow and regret, saying he had *"hoped to be able to do a resection but could not find even six inches."* I attempted to thank him for trying to help. Sister Paula Therese spoke to Doctor Rousselot, *"I never saw such a condition, Doctor."* He replied he had not either, except for one other case and he remarked to the Sisters of Charity, *"Remember Monsignor Bingham?"* I inquired how it could be we were not sooner aware of such a condition. He replied, *"Because the paralysis acted as a sort of anesthetic. Mother will have no pain but I do not believe she will last twelve hours and I think it will run down faster than that."* Then he motioned me to enter the operating room and the Supervisor said, *"Okay, Mother, everything is shut off now."* In the operating room were a patient of Doctor Rousselot's, Bishop Rada of Ecuador, Father Gilson, S.J., and another priest just finishing prayers for Mother, including the Apostolic Blessing.

They had given Mother block anesthesia, so she was fully conscious as I went to her side and patted her arm tied to the intravenous board. She said, *"I'm fine, everything will be all right."* We withdrew, standing outside until the Doctors finished their work, during which I was introduced to the Bishop (a three day post-operative) and the two priests. Doctor Rousselot took Bishop by the arm and told him he better get back to bed.

Soon we accompanied Mother on her stretcher down a few doors to the recovery room, where she was receiving blood in one arm and a solution in the other for about an hour. During this interval she recommended that the doctors, interns and nurses get some ice cream. She also asked for her leg brace so she could get up and out. Then the Sisters of Charity thoughtfully had Mother's bed brought from her room to avoid another move for her. All the while, for irrigation and control of vomiting, she had a Wagenstein tube in one nostril and one in the other supplying oxygen. Once in a while she would raise her free right arm to indicate she would like to have them removed, and Sister Rose Assunta would say, *"Just a while longer, Mother,"* and she would submit; otherwise, there was no sign of complaint.

In the afternoon Father General (Bishop Lane) arrived with Father Dietz, MM Bishop Lane said the prayers for the dying and gave Mother the Apostolic Blessing and very thoughtfully arranged with the hospital sisters for Father Dietz to remain there overnight in case of need. Monsignor Nelson also came. Early Saturday evening two cars arrived from the Motherhouse with a number of sisters, including the Council, Sister Annette and the Local Superiors.

A little later a small group of us softly sang the *Salve* at Mother's bedside. Sunday morning the sisters brought Father Cotta down, and later in the day a few of Mother's group arrived at the hospital. While Mother could speak, everyone in turn was asked, *"How are you?"*

Ellen went home to prepare supper and returned later with Frank with the news that Mother's nephew, Gerry Rogers, Paulist Seminarian, would be in from Washington on a night train. He reached the hospital about 1:00 a.m., and Mother asked him what he was doing here. He joined us in the vigil of prayers at her bedside. At about 9:00 p.m., his father Abe telephoned to ask if he should come down. I told him the doctor's prognosis. He and Ruth left Holbrook, MA, shortly before 1:00 a.m. and reached the hospital Sunday in time for a second Mass said by Father Dietz, and remained throughout the day. All three of them returned to the Motherhouse with us that evening. During the night, perspiration was profuse and Mother frequently asked her nurses to turn her. Saturday evening she asked Sister Regina Therese for a book. Sister asked, *"Detective Story?"* and Mother readily replied, *"Yes,"* but was, of course, in no way able to read.

Many others, including priests, relatives and friends, visited and prayed through Saturday afternoon and all day Sunday. Doctors were in frequently and Doctor Kennedy said, *"She was a great lady!"* When Abe and Ruth greeted her Sunday morning, she was a little excited but really relieved to have them come. Sister James very courageously spent most of Sunday at Mother's bedside saying Rosaries. At one point Mother said, *"Tell Sister James everything will be all right,"* and truly we all believe Mother is helping Sister to an admirable and edifying fortitude.

Early Sunday afternoon a change seemed to take place and during this time Doctor Sverdlik, the Director of Rehabilitation Therapy, for whom Mother had a great respect and admiration, came in and took her hand. All hearts ached to see the physical struggle she was making to greet him, and finally we caught a halting, *"How are you?"* He patted her hand and said, *"I am fine, Mother. Do not try to talk. It's how are you? Be quiet and try to rest."* Up to this time the demoral did not seem to afford much rest, so the resident doctor switched to morphine. From about 2:00 p.m., we all prayerfully waited for God's call, which came quietly after a few short struggles for breath at 5:18 p.m. As one of Mother's personal friends wrote, *"The right time never comes to part with those we love."*

ဆ ဆ ဆ

The following details are a continuation of Mother Mary Columba's Account

Events after Mother Mary Joseph's Death

Reporters, Funeral Arrangements

Reporters had been to the hospital and we learned next day that news of Mother's illness and passing went out over the radio Saturday and Sunday nights. On request a Sister of Charity called for me the Abbey Funeral Corporation on Madison Avenue of which the brother of Father McLarney, OP, is a member.

After my return Sunday evening, I telephoned Mother's sister, Elizabeth, Mrs. Novak, in Baltimore. She had been unable to get up before Mother's passing, but was aware of it as Ellen had called her and other members of the family. Ellen was a tower of strength and a wonderful tonic for all of us. Our ever generous sisters, especially those in the Secretariat, spent a good part of the night and the days following getting out notices by wire and mail and working out the many details needing to be covered. Sister Jeanne Marie and her assistants played a very comforting and helpful part of foreseeing and planning many details throughout the house. By wire we summoned the United States and Central American Superiors.

Telephone Call from Cardinal Spellman

About 10:45 p.m., Sunday, October 9, as I was retiring, the night phone rang. The voice announced, *"This is Cardinal Spellman. I suppose Mother Columba has gone to bed."* I replied, *"This is Mother Columba, Your Eminence."* He expressed his sympathy for us in Mother's death and said, *"I should like to come up and say Mass for her."* I told him that would be wonderful, etc. He continued, *"Would you like a Pontifical Requiem?"* I assured him we would be greatly honored and thanked him. He replied, *"Well, I had a great respect and admiration for her and this is the first time I have offered to say a Pontifical Mass, but there is no community for whom I have a higher esteem than yours."*

Selecting a Casket and Mr. Kado arrives from Los Angeles

Sisters Annette, Rose Assunta, Regina Therese and I went to the Abbey parlors on Monday morning to dress dear Mother and to select a casket. We chose a grey metal casket, lined with a soft gray *shirre* chiffon velvet. Pictures of this will go to you.

Mr. McLarney conducted everything in a most dignified manner and all his confreres were most cooperative in the special arrangements we wished to make for temporary internment of Mother's remains, pending transfer to the Motherhouse grounds before many months have passed. Mr. Kado, who flew here for the funeral with our Rosa from Los Angeles, worked in the afternoon on a landscape sketch for a cemetery-to-be, including a special placement of Mother's grave, which we hope to have enshrined.

Meeting Mother's Body

Father David I. Walsh thoughtfully came over Monday afternoon and arranged with Father Cotta the ceremony of meeting Mother's body which arrived about 5:00 p.m. Her Paulist nephew, Gerry, carried the processional cross and we all, with lighted candles, followed into the Novices' Chapel for the completion of the prayers.

There was some uncertainty as to who the visiting clergy might be, so Father General and Father Walsh thoughtfully relieved and assured me they would see that everything necessary in connection with the Pontifical Requiem Mass would be covered. All our Fathers were on call and in thoughtful attendance during Mother's repose here. As usual, our good Maryknoll Brothers were engaged as pall bearers.

Photos Taken, Procession Line, Father General's Homily

The Motherhouse News has brought you an account of the intervening days and of the Funeral Mass. The pictures taken of the chapel on this occasion will give you a fair idea of the great number of clergy (with a good sprinkling of purple), as well as Mother's relatives (most of those of the immediate family came) and friends. The line of cars in the funeral procession was rather impressive. A copy of Father General's fine eulogy has been prepared for each of you. Bishop Lane has instructed all the Fathers to offer for Mother all the suffrages granted to their own members.

Telegrams, Letters, Notes and Spiritual Offerings

Since the announcement of Mother's death went out there has been a flood of telegrams, letters, notes and spiritual offerings. Through tabulations we have reached a total of nearly two thousand Masses offered for her alone and I know there are many being said of which we have no record. We who were a part of the immediate family lived too close to Mother to realize fully the monumental character of her work which these spontaneous encomiums of admiration and praise highlight, coming as they do from people of all walks of life. We are compiling albums of pictures and noteworthy messages for posterity.

This letter is already lengthy and has been written in installments. It is now the Feast of All Saints and if you are ever to get this, I must bring it to a close.

Let me express again my deep appreciation of your precious notes of sympathy, loyalty and prayers. I am counting further on your generosity to let this most inadequate account of dear Mother's last days be my acknowledgment.

Know we shall all be mindful of Mother's last request through one of her nurses, Sister Rose Assunta,

Tell Mother Columba to ask the sisters to pray for me.
They will think I do not need prayers, but I do.

Lovingly,
Mother Mary Columba

ಐ   ಐ   ಐ

#27 ~ January 1956 Maryknoll Magazine

This was the last picture taken of Mother Mary Joseph by Sister M. Corde Lorang, less than a week before Mother died.

The Superior General's Corner

By
Bishop Raymond A. Lane, MM,
Superior General
of the Maryknoll Society

Someone has said:
Do not praise a woman until you have seen her daughters.

By that standard, Mother Mary Joseph was indeed great! Without her, thousands of young women could not have followed their foreign mission vocation. Without her, there would still be the fear and timidity of sending American sisters to faraway places, and women would be considered the weaker sex as far as foreign missions go. Without her, Maryknoll would not have advanced or grown as rapidly as has been the case. She was a fit instrument in the hands of God.

By indirection she influenced Father Walsh whose faith and loyal disciple she was at all times. She was God's gift, indeed, to him, to the Maryknoll Sisters, to the American sisterhoods and to the Church throughout the world. She should receive credit for stimulating vocations to American sisterhoods in general.

She made the idea popular in America that American womanhood in habits can give any service required by the least of Christ's brothers and sisters. It was something revolutionary in the concept of sisterhoods to see smiling faces of sisters in photographs, proving that they keep their individuality and permit grace to build on nature.

The Church has made Little Therese, who stayed in the Cloister in spite of a foreign-mission vocation, equal to St. Francis Xavier with the title, *Patroness of the Missions*. It may be, time will prove, that Mother Mary Joseph is the equal of any American missioner who ever left our shores.

The essence of the missionary vocation is undoubtedly contained in the paradox in the Gospel: *"Whoever loses one's life for my sake shall find it."* One of the very last things Mother did was something that brings out this very point. It was beautiful indeed in one who is the founder and the ideal of others.

Just a few hours before she passed away, she was struggling to say something. The mechanical contrivance in her mouth to help her condition was interfering. She seemed most anxious to speak to the doctor. Finally, after some effort, those around her were able to detect what she wanted to say and it was, *"How are you, doctor?"*

At the point of death, one dying usually holds the center of the drama and is made to feel the center. But here we have Mother Mary Joseph carrying out consistently her outstanding trait ~ thoughtfulness of others. It is a beautiful picture and a beautiful ideal.

+ Raymond A. Lane

೫ ೫ ೫

#28 ~ Among Mollie's Many Dear Friends

Harriet Shadd

In 1901, Harriet Shadd and Mollie had met their first day at Smith College at the Registrar's Office, where both had gone for the academic fine-tooth-combing for which the Registrar was well-known. Harriet, lonely and fearful, had responded with a full heart to Mollie's warm smile. They waited for each other and walked home together and so began a lasting friendship.

As Mollie's and Harriet's friendship ripened, Mollie wondered if Harriet would go from hurt to hurt, blocked from personal fulfillment by barriers not of her own making. Mollie had thought about Harriet a great deal. Although not as closely associated with this refined and vivacious young woman as with those in her own residence, Mollie had a special love for her.

Mollie had a revelation of what life was like for Harriet, who looked Italian or perhaps Jewish, with fine features and olive skin, but was neither. She was a Washingtonian of both white and Negro blood. What this meant to one of her gifts and means and opportunities had been partially disclosed at the time of the Junior Prom.

The Junior Prom was the one social affair at Smith in the early nineteen hundreds to which young men were invited. At other times, they might call under carefully specified conditions, but for a Smith young woman to go out riding unchaperoned was not allowed. As a result of restricted visiting privileges and being constantly chaperoned, the Junior Prom was an important event. Not to have an escort for the Prom was unthinkable.

One of Mollie's brothers was to accompany Harriet, but at very nearly the last minute Harriet came to beg off. A younger student from Washington who knew of Harriet's family had been to her to say, *"How can you go to the Prom with Mollie's brother? You mean to say they do not know? What an awful thing for you to do! If you do not tell them, I will."* Harriet came to see Mollie to let her know that she could not go to the dance.

Mollie, who was very intuitive, invited Harriet to sit down and share more with her. Harriet said that being of mixed blood, it was better for her not to go. Mollie would have nothing to do with this attitude, and encouraged Harriet to go to the dance as she was a special part of the group of friends.

The whole party closed ranks around Harriet both at the dance and on the next day's outing on which about a dozen of them went together. Always well dressed, Harriet looked charming and seemed especially happy when picnicking at Whately Glen. However, when it came time to take pictures and Mollie tucked Harriet's hand through her arm and drew her to her side, Harriet shrank behind her out of sight.

Since her recent insight into the revelation of Harriet's world, both inner and outer, Mollie felt not only compassion for her but a new admiration ~ for her courage, the integrity that had survived so many corroding experiences, the enduring impulse toward the best in life.

Harriet's Letter to Mother Mary Joseph in 1930

In a letter written to Mother Mary Joseph in 1930, Harriet was able to write, even if she had to put it lightly, some of the feelings that she had been unable to express when she was younger.

Dear Mollie:

I went back to Hampton for the reunion. It was my first return in a quarter of a century. I just made myself go back. I did not want to go. I had four such unhappy years at Smith that it never seemed possible I would willingly return.

You will probably wonder why I say that you are responsible for my return. Well, you are, Old Dear. As I look back on those first days in Hamp, yours was the first face that I remember. You were such a comfortable person, such an understanding friend. On one of our walks down Elm Street, I yelled at the sight of some caterpillars....You stopped short on the sidewalk and turning said to me, "Harriet, you should put your hand in a nest of caterpillars and let them crawl over your hand until you have broken yourself of this fear." I gasped at the thought and I have never physically had the courage to touch a caterpillar, but I have taken your advice in a good many instances and spiritually flung myself into a nest of beasties....My trip back to Northhampton was an excursion of this sort....Well, I had a glorious time and my one regret is that I did not see you.

When I was twenty-eight, I joined the Episcopal Church and at one time, Mollie, I seriously considered entering a sisterhood. I was so tired of the storm and stress of the world ~ this being a mixed blood in America is not always a bed of roses.

My love to you, dear, and if there is ever a chance of seeing you, please let me know.

Affectionately yours,
Harriet

Nearly twenty-five years later, they were still communicating with each other. Mother Mary Joseph wanted Harriet, who had been ill, to know the secret of her own peace and to share it with her to the full. In January 1954, Mother wrote to her old friend by hand, not an easy task for her anymore.

Dear Harriet,

I am wondering how you are and what you are doing. It is good to know that you will be yourself again and no need to worry.

It is two years now since I was stricken. I had a very great grace at that time. I was in the car when the stroke came. Very unusual ~ it came gradually and as I felt my tongue sort of rolling up, I said to the sister beside me, "I think I am having a stroke." And at the same time I said to God, "I do not know what is happening to me but I not only accept it as Your will, I wish to embrace it, no matter what it is." And ever since I have tried to love what God has sent me. It has made a very heavy cross light to carry and the days sweet instead of full of bitterness as they might have been. So sometimes when you are praying, thank God for me, please.

I am improving all the time, came back from the hospital just before Christmas. When you have a chance, write me about yourself.

Enclosed is the Pope's prayer for the Marian Year. May Our Lady bless you! Sister James sends greetings with mine. Love to you and your companions. God bless you. Mollie

Resources
The above Reflections were adapted from:
Maryknoll's First Lady by Jeanne Marie Lyons, MM.

ဢ   ဢ   ဢ

Julia Ward

*The following is adapted from reflections Mother Mary Joseph
gave to the Valley Park Novices in 1948, and the Teresian Diaries.*

Julia Ward's name is one that needs to be familiar to all of you. I first met her when we were in our little house at Hawthorne. Miss Ward had been a dressmaker in New York City, and a very successful one. She amassed quite a large fortune and had invested wisely. She did a great deal of work for the actresses, especially for Maude Adams. She was famous in making wardrobes for Broadway plays, living in Manhattan and having a Fashion Shop there. The name *"Ward"* on a theatre program meant something!

Miss Ward had very wide interests and had traveled much through Europe in her dressmaking business. She had never married; but she had many relatives depending on her. She became interested in the Propagation of the Faith. She was also interested in priests who were sick and had no place to go for rest and care. I do not know how many priests she sent away and cared for while they were getting well. She gave much to the Cenacle in New York City. When they bought their second house, she put in the new Chapel with all its furnishings. She put roof gardens on schools and gave playgrounds. No one but myself and her lawyer knew the extent of her charity. She had taken a fancy to me for some reason or other and used to ask my advice about her gifts, although I was very much younger than she.

When we moved to Maryknoll in Ossining, our house was in terrible condition. The floors were of rough boards. We had no screens. Miss Ward had good floors put in and the house screened and painted. She sent us much food. She it was who helped us design our habit.

Early in the summer of 1914, Father Walsh told us that Miss Ward, who was a great friend and benefactor of Maryknoll, was going to Europe and wanted me to go with her. I was not too well at the time and Father thought it would be a wonderful opportunity for me. With the approval of Father Walsh, Cardinal Farley and the Teresians, I went to Europe with her. It was a wonderful experience for me. We visited Paris and the Chateau country, Tours and Orleans, where Joan of Arc had lived.

By June 1914, Europe was seething. In July, there was a run on the banks and the people began to fear war. Finally, we got to Lourdes on the last train from Paris. We were in Lourdes on the day war was declared and heard the Mayor of the town in the public square read the mobilization orders from the government for the war that began in August.

Julia Ward was also President of the Catholic Women's Association (CWA), which had been founded by Mrs. Livingston in 1912. Both Julia and Mrs. Livingston are mentioned often in the early Teresian Diaries from 1912 onward. The CWA group visited Maryknoll annually with their substantial offerings of the year, until 1953 when it was phased out.

Through many years Miss Ward was our fairy godmother, as related throughout the pages of the *Distaff*. During our first decade in the Motherhouse, she had much illness. In 1932, following a series of attacks of a mysterious nature, she was taken to a neurological hospital. There her illness was diagnosed as a brain tumor, for which she underwent successful surgery. I visited her frequently during her slow recovery. She remained partially paralyzed. In August she came to the Motherhouse and stayed with us until the end of the year.

While she was with us, Sisters Michael Conlin and Cecilia Cruickshank occupied her apartment in New York city during the weeks they held our Christmas Sale in her building. For several years, during November and December, she gave us the use of her store for an Oriental Exhibit and Christmas Sale.

In August 1934, she sold her building on 48th Street and sent her furniture to the Motherhouse. After disposition of her home, Miss Ward with Sister Dominica Gallagher as nurse, occupied our Chaplain Suite, where part of her furniture had been placed. Throughout our first decade in the Motherhouse and later, up to the time of her death, Miss Ward was frequently with us. It was a privilege to be able to extend hospitality to this noble woman who had done so much both for the Maryknoll Society and for our own community, not only in the early days but down through the years. Later, she lived with a companion in New York City and then in Bayside, Long Island.

Miss Ward lost most of her fortune. After many years of suffering, she died in Bayside on December 2, 1950, as a Dominican Tertiary. She was buried in the Dominican habit which our Sister Ambrose Crawford had made for that purpose years earlier.

Julia Ward certainly did not go to God with empty hands. She had nothing to leave; but she gave lavishly while she had it. I encourage our community to pray for Miss Ward and to remember her great goodness to us!

Resources
Discourses of Mother Mary Joseph Rogers, MM, Volume IV, pp. 1431-1434, and the 1912-1916 Teresian Diaries

℘ ℘ ℘

Nellie O'Hara

Nellie was born in Belfast, Ireland, on May 24, 1888. She was the daughter of George O'Hara, from Ireland serving in the British Army and of Jane Oliver, from England. They had a large family of four sons and nine daughters. Nellie married young and had an early separation from her husband, who disappeared, leaving Nellie to care for their little daughter, Frances.

Later Nellie met Ted (Edmund Dance), a competent and quiet man who had in his youth served in the Merchant Marine and learned to be a good cook. Nellie and Ted were a compatible and contented couple and managed a small restaurant together. When Frances was old enough, she was enrolled in a Sisters' Boarding School.

Sometime later, Nellie's first husband, who was presumed dead, appeared. Nellie and Ted sought counsel from Paulist Father John Handly, famous for his missions and retreats. Under his guidance, they made the hard choice to separate, and become associated with a religious community. Father Handly was a good friend of Father James A. Walsh and also knew Mother Mary Joseph. After making arrangements with both of them, Nellie arrived at St. Teresa's Lodge on August 23, 1923. Ted joined the Maryknoll Brothers and eventually became Brother Mark, and was well regarded as a good community person and an able chef. Ted died at Los Altos, CA, March 3, 1943, and was buried there.

As an affiliate, Nellie brought with her an ability and willingness to turn her hand to many different tasks. She was blessed with a solid faith and a capacity to enjoy life. She had, besides, a dash of Irish exuberance with a touch of Irish melancholy, a sense of good humor and a flair for transforming ordinary occasions and commonplace events into startling happenings.

One of her early assignments was to the Minor Seminary, the Venard, outside Scranton, PA, to help Maryknoll Sisters in the daily preparation of meals for the Maryknoll Fathers, Brothers and young students, a considerable group.

In 1932, Nellie was Guest Mistress and lived now in the Motherhouse Guest Wing, near the 2nd floor tribune, and helped out where needed, especially with driving.

In 1935, Nellie went to Hawaii for a period of time to oversee the School Cafeteria in Honolulu. When she got to the train station, Nellie discovered that her pocketbook was still locked inside her room at the Motherhouse. Nellie telephoned Maryknoll and the operator, Sister Jane Frances Victory, who was also the official chauffeur, rushed from the switchboard, located the pocketbook, after getting the key to the room from the neighbor across the hall, ran downstairs, jumped into the car and rushed to the Station where, thanks to the three-minute holdup ~ due to Nellie's holding on to the conductor's suspenders to prevent him from giving the go-ahead signal ~ all ended happily with Nellie on her way!

The only time Nellie was away from the community was as a companion for Agnes Cogan, the partially invalid sister of Sister Mary de Paul Cogan.

As Nellie aged, so did her humor and she was heard saying to a Maryknoll Sister: *"Sometimes I just think that I will leave but then along comes one of those grand funerals and I decided to stay on and have one myself!"* Nellie died in our Nursing Home on June 11, 1985 at the age of 97 and had a grand funeral! She is buried in our cemetery.

Resources
The above Reflections were adapted from:
notes prepared by Sister Jeanne Marie Lyons, MM,
for Nellie O'Hara's Letter of Appreciation,
given by Sister Suzanne Moore, MM, Central Governing Board,
at the Mass of Resurrection in the Maryknoll Sisters
Chapel of the Annunciation on June 13, 1985.

80   80   80

#29 ~ Chronology
Heritage Reflection with Mollie

United with Mollie on the journey and in the grace of the Holy One,
who calls forth and nurtures our mission vocation ~
we remember, give thanks for and continue Mollie's Dream!

1876 September 28 - Mollie's Parents, Abraham Theobald Rogers and Mary Josephine Plummer, were married in St. Francis de Sales Church in Charlestown, MA.

1882 October 27 - Mollie, the 4th child, was born in Roxbury, MA. She was the first daughter in a family of 8 children ~ 5 boys and 3 girls: William (1877), Leo (1879), Edmund (Ned 1881), Mollie (1882), Elizabeth (1885), Louise (1888), John (1890) and Abe (1891).

1882 November 13 - Mollie was baptized *Mary Josephine* at St. Francis de Sales Church, Roxbury, MA.

1894 October 7 - Mollie was confirmed, choosing the name *Frances*, at the Church of St. Thomas, Jamaica Plain, MA, by Archbishop John J. Williams of Boston.

1888-1897 - Mollie attended Bowditch Grade School in Jamaica Plain, MA, a nine-year course.

1897-1901 - Mollie attended West Roxbury High School, Roxbury, MA, a three-year course, graduating in June 1900. Mollie was chosen the Class Speaker. Her talk was on *Toleration*. Mollie took the optional 4th year for college preparation, receiving a diploma on June 25, 1901.

1901-1905 - Mollie attended four years at Smith College in Northampton, MA, graduating on June 18, 1905, with a Bachelor of Arts Degree in Zoology. As a Junior, Mollie experienced the enthusiasm of the Protestant students at Smith who signed a pledge to go for a period of time to China as foreign missioners. Mollie wrote: *"Something—I do not know how to describe it— happened to me....I passed quickly through the campus....and across to the Church, where....I measured my faith and expression of it by the sight I had just witnessed....From that moment I had a work to do, little or great God alone knew."*

1905-1906 - Mollie spent a year at Boston Normal School in a special section for College Graduates and received a Teaching Certificate.

1906 Fall-1908 June - Mollie had a Fellowship at Smith College to assist in the Zoology Department and to purse her Master's Degree.

1906 - Miss Elizabeth Deering Hanscom, a Faculty member at Smith College, inspired and influenced Mollie to start a Mission Study Club at Smith for Catholic young women. This Mission Club led Mollie to Father James Anthony Walsh (JAW), Director of the Society of the Propagation of the Faith in the Boston Archdiocese. Mollie corresponded with Father Walsh in October, and in December met him at his Office. He showed Mollie the galley sheets for the first issue of *The Field Afar* magazine, to be published in January 1907. Mollie devoted all her free time assisting Father Walsh in editing, translating, writing for *The Field Afar*, as well as organizing his mission photo collection.

1908 Fall-1912 June - Mollie taught at the Boston Public Elementary and High Schools.

1910 September 15 - Mollie made a Formal Resolve to devote herself to mission work.

1911 June 29 - Maryknoll Society Foundation Day.

1912 January 6 - The three secretaries, Mary Louise Wholean, Sara Teresa Sullivan and Mary Augustine Dwyer arrived at Hawthorne, NY, to assist Father Walsh, receiving $25 a month each for their services.

1912 July - Mollie arrived at Hawthorne to help temporarily with the work, creating an atmosphere that was unifying and personally freeing for the togetherness of Mary Louise, Sara, Mary Augustine and Nora Shea. Mary Louise wrote in the Diary: *"These happy days we find Mollie as generous, as resourceful, as organist and leading soprano, as cook, as shampooist, as gardener. She did every kind of work imaginable."*

1912 August 14 - Father Walsh brought Mollie and Monsignor John J. Dunn, Director of the Society of the Propagation of the Faith of the New York Archdiocese, to visit the *Hill Top Farm* on Pinesbridge Road near Ossining, a property up for sale by a certain Mr. Law.

1912 August 17 - In the morning, Mother Mary Alphonsa of the Dominican Sisters in Hawthorne gave $2,000 to Mollie as a gift which made it possible for Mollie to join the secretaries in September.

1912 August 17 - In the afternoon, Mollie with Father Walsh as Chauffeur, Mr. Fitzpatrick and Mr. Broderick (Realtors), and Mr. Ewing (Lawyer), went to White Plains. Mollie, as Miss Rogers from Jamaica Plain, MA, purchased the property from Mr. Law ~ 93 acres for $44,500. The property was then deeded by Mollie to the Catholic Foreign Mission Society for one dollar. When Mr. Law discovered that Miss Rogers bought the land for the Society, he wrote a very gentlemanly letter in which he said that he welcomes Maryknoll and our influence.

1912 September 9 - Mollie arrived at Hawthorne from St. Thomas Parish in Jamaica Plain, MA, with Margaret Ann Shea. Mollie said to Margaret: *"Let's just go together and see what God has in store for us!"*

1912 September 15 - Mollie, now called Mary Joseph, was chosen by the secretaries as *Head of the Household* by unanimous vote. Mollie wrote this note to them: *"I want you to know how wholly I belong to you in every hour of the day and night, to serve you, to love you, to watch over you and with you, under the guidance of the Holy Spirit, for of myself I can do nothing. I offer to this work the service of my entire being."* (September 15 is also the 2nd Anniversary of Mollie's commitment to devote herself to mission work.)

1912 September 18 - The Fathers, Brothers and Seminarians moved from Hawthorne to Maryknoll. Before long, the Society's cook disappeared, and Mollie, with the help of Hannah, the secretaries' cook, went to Maryknoll Seminary to do the cooking till October 17, when a new cook relieved her.

1912 October 15 - Mollie was already at Maryknoll overseeing the Society's kitchen. Mary Louise Wholean (Sr. M. Xavier), Margaret Ann Shea (Sr. M. Gemma) and Anna Agnes Towle (Sr. Anna Maria) moved from Hawthorne to Maryknoll. Then on October 16, Sara Teresa Sullivan (Sr. Teresa), Nora Frances Shea (Sr. Theophane) and Mary Augustine Dwyer (who left in 1916) joined the secretaries at St. Teresa's Lodge. After the secretaries were settled at St. Teresa's Lodge, Mill Hill Father McCabe, who had been helping at the Maryknoll Seminary, sent a postcard from England to them. He addressed it to *The Teresians*. The name took hold immediately and the secretaries, already dedicated to St. Teresa of Avila, became *The Teresians of Maryknoll*.

1913 May 5 - A simple Reception of the Teresians, each wearing a gray uniform, took place. On May 29, the Cincture was added.

1916 January - The Teresians voted whether to become Carmelites, Franciscans or Dominican Tertiaries. They chose to be Dominican Tertiaries, and 17 Teresians were officially enrolled on March 7 in the Dominican 3rd Order.

1917 February 19 - Sister M. Xavier Wholean, at the age of 35, was the first Maryknoller to die. She was one of the three who came to Hawthorne on January 6, 1912, and she wrote the first Teresian Diaries.

1917 March 25 - All Teresians wearing the cincture received a silver Chi Rho ring, symbolic of the work to which they had dedicated their lives. The rings were designed by Maryknoll Sister Elenita Barry's Mother, Rose, who loved Mollie and made the rings for her as a gift. The rings were blessed by Father James A. Walsh. Permission was received from Rome to organize as a Society of Pious Women, but the Teresians could not yet take Vows. They began to call each other *Sister* and were known as *Dominican Tertiaries of Maryknoll*.

1918 July 16 - Mollie and twelve others made their vows privately to Father Charles Callan, OP, who was one of the teachers at the Seminary.

1919 July 15 - Sister Fidelia, OP, arrived from Sinsinawa, WI, to assist in the Novitiate till June 22, 1924.

1919 September 12 - Father Price died in China from a ruptured appendix.

1920 February 14, Canonical Foundation Day - The Teresians received approval from Rome to be a Diocesan Congregation. Monsignor John J. Dunn of the New York Archdiocese telephoned this good news on February 12, and the official document from the Archdiocese was dated February 14, and was received a few days later. Mary Joseph was appointed by Archbishop Hayes as Superior till the 1st elective Chapter in 1925.

1920 April 8 - Maryknoll Sisters began in Los Angeles, CA, and on May 30 in Seattle, WA, ~ both serving the Japanese people.

1920 July 2 - Maryknoll Sisters were recognized by Father Louis Theissling, the Master General of the Order of Friars Preachers, as a true member of the Dominican Family via Bishop McNicholas, OP.

1921 February 15 - Mother Mary Joseph and 20 other sisters made 1st Profession of Vows in the Chapel at St. Teresa's at Maryknoll, NY. On March 19 and April 13, 1921, two sisters in Los Angeles, CA, and two in Seattle, WA, also made their 1st Profession with Mother present.

1921 September 12 - Six Maryknoll Sisters: M. Paul McKenna, Superior; M. Rose Leifels, M. Lawrence Foley, M. Barbara Froehlich, M. Imelda Sheridan and M. Monica Moffatt left for Hong Kong and Yeungkong. They docked in Kowloon on November 3, and arrived in Yeungkong, South China, November 20.

1923 - The Maryknoll Sisters were housed in five dwellings at Maryknoll, NY: St. Teresa's Lodge, St. Joseph's (a converted barn), Dormitories in *The Field Afar* Building (now Walsh Building), Rosary House (pro-Seminary) and St. Michael's (Carriage House). The Chapel was now a separate building called St. Martha's.

1923 September 11 - Mother Mary Joseph leaves for her first Visitation to Asia, returning in March 1924.

1924 February 11 - Mother Mary Joseph's Final Profession in Korea with Sister Paul McKenna. Father Patrick Byrne, MM, presided.

1925 May 6 - 1st General Chapter at which Mother Mary Joseph was elected unanimously as Mother General; she also acted as Local Superior until 1931.

1927 June - The Maryknoll Society purchased the Tompkins' Estate across the way from their present property, which extended from the highest point in Westchester to Brookside Lane. On August 15, Father James A. Walsh blessed the family dwelling on the highest point naming it *Regina Coeli*. This became part of the Sisters' Novitiate.

1928 November 7 - Maryknoll Sisters purchased from the Society 53 acres of the former Tompkins' Estate, including *Regina Coeli* hilltop, and the land on which the Center was built. The Society retained the southern portion of 8.86 acres. In July 1945, on our inquiry of the Society to purchase this remaining portion, including Potter's House, they made a gift of it to us for past services rendered to the Society by the sisters. In the 1970's, Potter's House was re-bought by the Maryknoll Society.

1929 September 15 - Auxiliary Bishop John Dunn of New York Archdiocese presided at the groundbreaking for the Sisters' Center.

1931 July 9 - 2nd General Chapter at which Mother Mary Joseph was re-elected unanimously.

1932 March 3 - We moved into the newly built Center. Mother saw the move from the Seminary grounds to the Center as marking *"a very final step towards a new phase of our life."*

1932 October 3 - Among the decisions of the 1931 Chapter was the approval for the Cloister (now called Contemplative Community) to begin as an integral part of the Congregation.

1933 June 29 - Father James A. Walsh was ordained a Bishop in Rome. He died at Maryknoll on April 14, 1936.

1937 July - The 3rd General Chapter at which Bishop James E. Walsh, the new Superior General, spoke of the Maryknoll Sisters as *actual missioners* rather than *helpers of missionaries*. Mother Mary Joseph was unanimously re-elected to a 3rd term of office in the form of a *postulation*. It was granted readily by Cardinal Hayes, his not knowing a *postulation* had to go to Rome. However, the fact that he approved the *postulation*, Rome would ordinarily approve it.

1946 July - At the 4th General Chapter, Mother Mary Joseph was elected as Mother General in the form of a *postulation*. In a reflective letter, dated December first, she communicated that on November 30, Cardinal Spellman of New York told her *"to refuse her election"* which involved a fourth term, and *"call an elective chapter."* Mother said: *"We can accept this as an act of obedience, or embrace it as an act of Love, facing this change with joy in doing God's will."*

1947 January 2 - Delegates returned to the Center and elected Mother Mary Columba to succeed Mother Mary Joseph.

1954 December 12 - Maryknoll Sisters became a Pontifical Congregation, and our name was changed from Foreign Mission Sisters of St. Dominic to Maryknoll Sisters of St. Dominic.

1955 October 9 - Mother Mary Joseph died peacefully at the age of 73 at St. Vincent's Hospital, NYC, at 5:18 p.m., surrounded by her Community.

₰ ₰ ₰

As long as there is a Maryknoll Sister
left in the world with a heart to love
and a will to serve,
Mollie's spirit and dream
continue to live on in the world!
Adapted from Sister Jeanne Marie's *Maryknoll's First Lady*

#30 ~ Three Honorary Degrees Received by Mother Mary Joseph

May 29, 1945
Regis College, founded in 1927
by the Congregation of the Sisters of St. Joseph of Boston,
presented Mother Mary Joseph with a Doctor of Laws Degree.
This was the first honorary degree in the history of Regis College,
and it was the 25th Anniversary of the Maryknoll Sisters
being canonically recognized as a Religious Congregation by Rome.

November 5, 1949
Trinity College in Washington, DC,
(now Trinity Washington University)
founded in 1897 by the Sisters of Notre Dame de Namur,
presented Mother Mary Joseph
with an Honorary Doctor of Laws Degree.

June 3, 1950
Smith College founded in 1871 in Northampton, MA,
presented Mother Mary Joseph with a
Doctor of Humane Letters Degree
on the 45th anniversary of her graduation.
Mother was the first and only sister
to be so honored by Smith College.
Among old friends present was
Miss Elizabeth Deering Hanscom.

৪০   ৪০   ৪০

#31 ~ Bibliography

Maryknoll Sisters ~ A Pictorial History,
by Sister Mary Francis Louise, MM, 1962, E. P. Dutton & Company, Inc., New York

Maryknoll's First Lady,
by Jeanne Marie Lyons, MM, 1964, Dodd, Mead & Company, New York

Into the Heart of Mission,
Booklet on the Contemplative Community,
by Madeline McHugh, MM, 1982, Maryknoll Contemplative Community,
Maryknoll, NY, 10545

To the Uttermost Parts of the Earth,
The Spirit and Charism of Mary Josephine Rogers,
by Camilla Kennedy, MM, 1987, The Maryknoll Sisters, Maryknoll, NY 10545

Maryknoll in China, A History: 1918-1955,
by Jean-Paul Wiest, 1988, Orbis Books, Maryknoll, NY 10545

Hearts on Fire, The Story of the Maryknoll Sisters,
by Penny Lernoux, with Arthur Jones and Robert Ellsberg,
1993, and Centenary Edition, 2012, Orbis Books, Maryknoll, NY 10545

On the Threshold of the Future,
The Life and Spirituality of Mother Mary Joseph Rogers,
Founder of the Maryknoll Sisters,
by Claudette LaVerdiere, MM, 2011, Orbis Books, Maryknoll, NY 10545

The Spirituality of Mollie Rogers,
Founder of the Maryknoll Sisters Congregation,
by Elizabeth E. Carr, Ph.D., 2012, The Maryknoll Sisters, Maryknoll, NY 10545

As One Lamp Lights Another,
The Life and Story of Mother Mary Joseph,
by Barbara Hendricks, MM, 2012, The Maryknoll Sisters, Maryknoll, NY 10545

Maryknoll Sisters in the 20th Century
Preaching by Living Justice,
by Bernice Kita, MM, 2013, The Maryknoll Sisters, Maryknoll, NY 10545

Maryknoll Mission Archives,
Maryknoll, NY 10545

ℰ ℰ ℰ

34237667R00110

Made in the USA
Charleston, SC
02 October 2014